Where do all the paperclips go?

Where do all the paperclips go?

... and 127 other business and career conundrums

By Steve Coomber & Marc Woods

CAPSTONE

BICENTENNIAL
1807
WILEY
2007
BICENTENNIAL

First published 2007 by:
Capstone Publishing Ltd. (a Wiley Company)
The Atrium, Southern Gate, Chichester, PO19 8SQ, UK.
www.wileyeurope.com
Email (for orders and customer service enquires): cs-books@wiley.co.uk

Other Wiley Editorial Offices
John Wiley & Sons Inc., 111 River Street, Hoboken, NJ 07030, USA
Jossey-Bass, 989 Market Street, San Francisco, CA 94103–1741, USA
Wiley-VCH Verlag GmbH, Boschstr. 12, D-69469 Weinheim, Germany
John Wiley & Sons Australia Ltd, 42 McDougall Street, Milton, Queensland 4064, Australia
John Wiley & Sons (Asia) Pte Ltd, 2 Clementi Loop #02–01, Jin Xing Distripark, Singapore 129809
John Wiley & Sons Canada Ltd, 22 Worcester Road, Etobicoke, Ontario, Canada M9W 1L1
Wiley also publishes its books in a variety of electronic formats. Some content that appears in print may not be available in electronic books.

Library of Congress Cataloging-in-Publication Data

Coomber, Stephen.
 Where do all the paperclips go-- and 127 other business and career conundrums / by Steve Coomber & Marc Woods.
    p. cm.
 Includes index.
 ISBN 978-1-84112-801-6
1. Vocational guidance--Miscellanea. 2. Career development--Miscellanea. 3. Business--Miscellanea. 4. Entrepreneurship--Miscellanea. 5. Industrial management--Miscellanea. I. Woods, Marc. II. Title.
 HF5381.C6874 2007
 650.1--dc22
                        2007029112

Anniversary Logo Design: Richard J. Pacifico

Set in Meta by Sparks, Oxford – www.sparks.co.uk
Printed and bound in the UK by TJ International Ltd, Padstow, Cornwall

This book is printed on acid-free paper responsibly manufactured from sustainable forestry in which at least two trees are planted for each one used for paper production. Substantial discounts on bulk quantities of Capstone Books are available to corporations, professional associations and other organizations. For details telephone John Wiley & Sons on (+44) 1243–770441, fax (+44) 1243 770571 or email corporatedevelopment@wiley.co.uk

Contents

Acknowledgements   *vi*

Introduction   *vii*

Section 1: Learning the ropes   1

Section 2: Getting the job done   25

Section 3: Working with others   53

Section 4: Climbing the ladder   79

Section 5: Rags to riches   101

Section 6: Happiness and health   123

Section 7: Department of miscellany   145

Section 8: Breaking free   177

Index   *203*

Acknowledgements

As always, thanks are due. Not least to Petra for, amongst many other things, managing to make some sense out of our answers in the form of illustrations; to Claire, Poppy and Myles, for their patience; and to John Moseley at Wiley: Capstone, who does such a great job there, and all the Capstone team.

Introduction

What this book is not

This book is not intended to advance new management theory, construct business models, or serve as a text for MBA students. There are no matrices, dashboards, graphs, spreadsheets, tables, PowerPoint slides, charts, tools, formulae, indigestible research reports, white papers, green papers, working papers or very long words.

What this book is

This book is written in a way that means you don't have to re-read the same passage three times before you understand it. It's short-ish, and full of interesting work-related information that you can read in ten-minute stints.

Why did we decide to write it?

Because the world of work is actually quirky, surprising, entertaining, and full of fascinating questions, like: where do all the paperclips go?

1.   Where do all the paperclips go?

The first bent-wire paperclip was patented in 1867 and, since then, dozens of different varieties have been designed to help hold papers together. It is estimated that 20 million paperclips are sold each year in America alone. Yet it seems that we still need help in getting organised.

Fast Company magazine stated that 48 per cent of American executives admit to having a messy desk but claim to know where everything is. By contrast, 12 per cent say that, although their desk appears organised, they have no idea where to find anything. Executives can waste up to six weeks a year searching for lost documents. Thankfully there are some simple things you can do to organise your office.

Get your desk under control

- If you don't use it everyday it doesn't need to be on your desk.
- Have a system for your incoming documents.
- Don't procrastinate. If you have picked up a document and decided what to do with it don't put it back in your in-tray. You will only have to pick it out again.

File don't pile

- Have a similar system for both computerised and paper-based files.
- Create an index for your filing system and check it before creating a new file to avoid making duplicates.
- Typically the most relevant document is the most recent. Within each file, store the most recent papers at the front.

Use your time wisely

- Break larger projects into smaller ones that are easier to manage and delegate.
- Know where you are in your diary and use it to plan your tasks.
- Interruptions happen. When you are allocating time to tackle a task, don't forget to factor in some extra for distractions and information gathering.

As for the missing paperclips, we know where some of them have gone.

In 1998, David Smith, an assistant principal at the Whitwell Middle School in Tennessee, suggested that they could use the events of the Holocaust as the basis for teaching tolerance within the school. Having difficulty in comprehending the enormity of the Holocaust, the students decided to collect six million paperclips to represent the estimated six million Jews killed between 1939 and 1945.

At first it was a slow process, but after receiving some publicity in the media millions of paperclips were sent to the school. Eleven million are now displayed in a rail car that was originally used to transport the prisoners to concentration camps; an additional eleven million paperclips are incorporated in a sculpture that stands next to it.

Section 1: Learning the ropes

- What is the best job in the world?
- Is your business card up to scratch?
- Have you ever lied on your CV?
- How strong are your old school ties?
- What will you be asked at your interview?
- What are you worth in the job market?
- How reliable are first impressions?
- Why are manhole covers round?
- What is the world's most dangerous job?
- Are you in the wrong place or are you the wrong Guy?
- What makes an organisation a great place to work?
- Have you got staying power?
- Do you have network *nous*?
- Should you get a mentor?
- Are you afraid of your job?

2.   What is the best job in the world?

Picking the best job in the world is very much a subjective task. If you are partial to a glass of Sauvignon Blanc with your lunch, a Gran Reserva Rioja with your evening meal and a sip of Château d'Yquem before bedtime then *you* may consider being a wine taster as the best job in the world.

Or perhaps you are the life and soul of the party, and can make anything you talk about sound funny. In that case, being a stand-up comedian may be your idea of the best job in the world.

However, regardless of the subjective nature of the task, we decided on the following 'best jobs in the world'.

3rd

For the anally retentive, obsessive compulsives amongst you, the people who like shiny, pristine surfaces, untouched and unmarked, we have the job for you. When the laughter and hollering has subsided and you can no longer hear the sound of steel cutting through ice, you can put order back into the world. Yes, you can become a Zamboni driver. Invented in 1949 by Frank J. Zamboni, who was born rather appropriately in Eureka, Utah, these are the little machines that glide over ice rinks resurfacing them.

2nd

What better way to spend your time than by helping save the lives of others? It may take you up to 14 years to qualify as a brain surgeon, and you still won't receive the largest remuneration, but the job satisfaction of helping others will be immense.

1st

If you were brought up catching and throwing, kicking and hitting or running and jumping, then the life of a professional sports person may be the thing for you. The chance to be paid to be fit, travel around the world and enjoy your sport may be just what you are looking for. And if you are good enough to be one of the best in the world at a sport that receives a lot of media coverage, you might earn a lot of money too. The top earners in golf, motorsport, basketball, tennis and football all earn tens of millions of pounds each year. Then, when you retire, and if you are capable of stringing a few words together, you might get asked to talk about the sport you love as a TV pundit.

As you might expect, there is no shortage of surveys on the best job in the world, none of which (to our knowledge) feature Zamboni drivers. What is interesting is how childhood aspiration rarely meets reality. In a survey for Career builder.com and Walt Disney, conducted by Harris Interactive, 84 per cent of people polled were not in their dream job.

Not that surprising when you consider the lofty ambitions of those surveyed. Thirty-three per cent of administrative professionals wanted to be princesses and 22 per cent of manufacturing workers dreamed of being cowboys. Over half of doctors and lawyers, and 24 per cent of teachers, wanted to be the US President.

3.   Is your business card up to scratch?

'Look at that subtle off-white colouring, the tasteful thickness of it ... oh my God, it even has a watermark.' Patrick Bateman, played by Christian Bale in the movie *American Psycho*, clearly suffered from, amongst other things, business card envy.

For people like Patrick Bateman, the look and feel of a business card is just as important as what is on it. Should the lettering of your name be embossed? Or perhaps the card should have a matt finish with spot UV high gloss details? The options are endless.

Of course you have decided on the content and set out your name, business, job title and contact details, but what else do you need to consider?

You could choose the quirky route and contact crazeydollars.com, who will print your information on a 'million dollar sizzle bill'; or perhaps your line of work calls for something a little more technologically advanced, and you may want a CD-Rom business card capable of storing videos clips, sound bites and information on all your products.

Once you have your new cards, the next decision is what to carry them in. After all, the eyes of your new contacts and potential business associates are on you as you pick out your card for them.

For £100 plus, a Swarovski crystal business cardholder studded with hundreds of pink crystals can be yours. Or if shiny bling is not your thing, maybe a Louis Vuitton monogrammed canvas cardholder with cross-grain leather lining. Or perhaps a sterling silver case from Tiffany & Co. is more your style.

Of course the whole point of having a business card is so that you can press it into the sweaty palm of a potential business associate. And, at this crucial moment, it is surprisingly easy to come unstuck. Some experts suggest that you should pass your card to someone once a business meeting has drawn to its conclusion. Others would say never offer your card until it is asked for.

In Oman, if you do offer your card to someone it should ideally have an Arabic translation on one side; likewise there should be a Russian translation when you are doing business in Russia.

In Japan, there is a specific way of exchanging business cards – a process called *meishi*. Business meetings cannot begin until *meishi* has been completed. Both hands should be used to present your card, which should be printed in both languages. Crucially, on receiving your counterpart's business card, it is important to make a show of examining it before placing it carefully on the table.

If, as in *American Psycho*, your business associate appears to be overly envious of your card, don't turn your back on them.

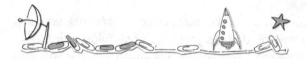

4.   Have you ever lied on your CV?

Is your CV more a work of fiction than an accurate appraisal of your skills and experience? Perhaps you have deviated from the truth in the hope that it gives you an edge, or to hide something from a perspective employer. If that is the case, then you are not alone.

A survey conducted by recruitment site monster.co.uk revealed that 40 per cent of respondents had lied about the reasons they left their job, 18 per cent about their current salary and 10 per cent about their qualifications. Only a third of people produce an entirely truthful CV.

With the power of the internet, it has become increasingly easy for employers to check up on applicants, so not only may you find yourself out of your depth and in the wrong job but, if discovered, you run the risk of tarnishing your reputation. Don't think that just because that falsified CV has long since been banished to the bottom of the filing cabinet you will automatically be safe.

David Edmondson, Chief Executive of Radio Shack, the third-largest electronics retailer in America, claimed to have received a degree at the Pacific Coast Baptist Bible College in California. Twelve years later, the error was uncovered by a newspaper. Edmondson subsequently resigned from his job and the substantial salary that went with it.

Singapore-based executive Patrick Imbardelli was due to be appointed to the main board of InterContinental, when the company learned there was a discrepancy on his CV. He did not have a number of degrees he claimed to have completed, including an MBA. Despite 25 years' experience in the tourism industry, over six years' experience with the company, working as Managing Director for the Asia Pacific region, and having been named Asia Pacific Hotelier of the Year 2006, Imbardelli was left with little choice but to resign.

While resignation doesn't automatically ensue, discovery of CV discrepancies can do untold damage to reputations and careers. James Gulliver, the former head of the Argyll drinks group, claimed in his *Who's Who* entry to have graduated with an MBA from Harvard. It turned out to be a fiction – something that came to light during a £2.3 billion takeover battle between Guinness and Argyll for Scottish whisky group, Distiller's. Some considered the revelation and ensuing damage to Gulliver's credibility to have affected the company's chances of success – it lost out to Guinness.

Be warned, the CV police are watching.

5.   How strong are your old school ties?

The 'old school tie effect' refers to the social and economic benefits of attending the 'right' school or university. Historically, the class system within the UK has reinforced its stranglehold, but is the knot slipping for the old school tie?

Apparently not. In 2006, the Sutton Trust reported that more than half of Britain's most influential journalists came from the seven per cent of the population who attended the elite educational facilities, as did seven out of ten barristers. Taking a look at politics, a third of MPs, in the highest positions, come from the elite institutions. In fact, since 1945, seven out of twelve prime ministers have been Oxford graduates; only three – Winston Churchill, James Callaghan and John Major – didn't have a degree (and Gordon Brown went to Edinburgh University).

John Major even tried to use an 'old school tie' jibe against the better-educated Tony Blair during the 1996 general election. In an attempt to portray himself as the decent ordinary man who had risen to the top, he played the class card against Blair by coining the phrase 'New Labour, Old School Tie'. Three terms of office later, Mr Blair left Number 10 Downing Street and few people referred to his educational background (or, indeed, his tie).

Of course, actually wearing an old school tie is probably not going to make that much of a difference. If your interviewer went to the same school as you, he will have seen it on your CV long before you make it into the room. Some decisions and assumptions about your character are made before you arrive.

Today, a far more overt way to leverage your old school network is on the internet, by using networking websites such as Facebook. Launched by Harvard graduate Mark Zuckerberg in February 2004, the Facebook site had profiles from 85 per cent of all college students in the US within 18 months. By its third year, Facebook had 25 million users worldwide.Although anybody can now join, at first people could only register if they belonged to a supported school, college or company. With its Ivy League roots, Facebook has proved a useful social networking tool for many. In the UK, it is proving especially popular with the 'old school tie' universities.

6.   What will you be asked at your interview?

Your alarm clock didn't go off because you hadn't set it properly, you had to run for the bus, stand up all the way and run to your interview. As you burst through the door, you notice how badly your shirt is sticking to your back and remember that, in your panic this morning, you forgot to put on any deodorant. And that's when you really start to sweat, as interviews can be nerve-wracking experiences.

An ABC News viewer told of a situation she found herself in during one interview.

'I was deposited in a room with the four folks who were to conduct the interview. The first person pulled out a list of questions and asked me a dozen or so. I answered them all without any trouble while the four of them listened intently. Then the second interviewer pulled out her list and asked the *exact same questions*, word for word. At first I thought it was a joke, but she kept asking. What was I to do? I answered them all again. Then the third person, and the fourth, asked the identical questions yet again. Maybe they were trying to judge my consistency, but it was a very uncomfortable interview and a strange way to treat a prospective employee.'

Interviews come in all shapes and sizes, but the well-prepared candidate is usually able to cope. There are a whole host of websites giving lists of possible interview questions which, as a rough guide, fall into five groups: about yourself; about your old job; about the new job; about the future; and then left field, surreal ones.

Handle the tough ones well – such as: 'How do you handle stress and pressure?'; 'What are your weaknesses and how do you work to overcome them?'; 'What was your greatest achievement and how did you accomplish it?'; 'Are you overqualified for this job?' – and the rest should be easy.

Of course, once you have sat through an interview, you may decide that the job isn't quite right for you. When the BBC asked for people to write in with their interview stories, they received the following:

'I had a job interview in which the interviewer asked me to "name three things you are not". Having quickly formed the conclusion throughout the interview that the company wasn't for me, the only reply I could think of was ... "Interested in this".'

7.   What are you worth in the job market?

The inclination is to answer: whatever market forces determine. The truth is not that simple, though.

To begin with, there are various government interventions that interfere with market forces. In the UK the minimum wage, set at £5.35 in 2006, means that – in theory – no worker should be paid less than that sum per hour.

Global economics and market forces do mean, however, that wages for similar activities vary widely from one country to the next. So in the UK, a newly qualified nurse might expect to earn about £19,000, while in India they would earn a starting salary of less than £1500 a year. Similarly, software developers in the UK are paid about £20,000 as graduates, but in India their starting salary is substantially lower at around £2000.

Anecdotal reports suggest that an influx of people from new EU member countries in recent years has maintained a downward pressure on wages in many sectors (for example, the construction sector).

At the other end of the pay scale to the minimum wage, CEO salaries continue their inexorable rise to stratospheric levels. According to statistics from the US Congressional Budget Office, between 1978 and 2005 CEO pay increased 35-fold to nearly 262 times the average worker's pay. Other research puts the ratio in the 400-times-average-earnings bracket. Average salaries at the top of the corporate hierarchy in the top 500 US companies are $10.9 million, and in the UK FTSE 100 close to £3 million.

And there is little indication that such salary increases depend solely on performance; in many cases, CEOs appear to benefit even if there is average performance or worse. The argument in support of such substantial salaries is that companies have to pay 'the going rate' to get the appropriate level of talent. Interestingly, though, while organisations are happy to outsource jobs to take advantage of labour cost differentials, there doesn't seem to be much of a move to outsource the CEO role in the same way. In 2005, for example, the average compensation of a CEO in Germany was something like a third of that of a CEO of a similar-sized company in the US. So why aren't US companies rushing to hire German CEOs?

For the average Joe, finding out your worth in the job market has never been easier. Forget scouring the job ads for positions similar to your own – it usually says 'salary on application' anyway. Just surf the internet and look for specialist salary comparison websites like salary.com or salaryexpert.com, or job websites like, totaljobs.com or monster (.com and .co.uk). Be warned though: it can make depressing reading.

8.   How reliable are first impressions?

'You never get a second chance to make a good first impression.' How many times have you heard that before? The reality, however, while a little less quotable, is a lot scarier.

In the early 1990s, Harvard University psychologist Nalini Ambady conducted an experiment into the nonverbal aspects of teaching. The idea was to get people to judge the effectiveness of teaching fellows by viewing minute-long video clips of the teachers with the sound off. The problem was, she only had ten-second clips with the teachers on their own in the frame – thus eliminating bias via the reactions of students in the background. Ambady went ahead anyway.

From a 'first impressions' perspective, the results were alarming. Despite the brief ten-second clip, the observers had no problem rating the teaching fellows on a fifteen-item checklist. The same applied with a five-second clip, and a two-second clip. If that wasn't bad enough, Ambady asked students to evaluate the same teachers after a semester spent in the same room observing the teaching fellows at close quarters. The results of the video observers and the students showed a high correlation: the verdicts on the teaching staff were virtually the same. Two seconds or several months? It makes no odds.

As for the mix of how we make an impression, 55 per cent comes through body language, 38 per cent from the tone, speed and inflection of our voice and only 7 per cent from what we're actually saying.

Fortunately, there is other research that suggests you might have up to four minutes to make an impression. In which case we suggest, other than giving some thought to the challenge, two things to focus on:

Try to remember people's names. We can all improve our memories. Dave Thomas, a fireman from Halifax, decided on a whim to improve his rather average memory. Two years later he was said to have one of the most powerful memories in the world, accomplishing feats such as memorising a shuffled pack of cards in 90 seconds and reciting 22,500 digits of the number *pi*. Although there is no need for you to take it that far!

Maintain steady eye contact. Steady eye contact shows that you are confident and alert to others around you. That's why expert advice has it that, should you ever come face to face with a mountain lion, you should give the animal the opportunity to move on, slowly backing away, but maintaining eye contact. Note, however, that unlike humans and mountain lions, brown bears don't like this as much; if you happen upon a brown bear, keep an eye on them, but avoid direct eye contact.

9.   Why are manhole covers round?

You may think that the days of surreal interview questions have passed; a fad that disappeared along with excessively large shoulder pads and mobile phones that still had to be hardwired to the dashboard of your car. Well think again.

Some universities are famous for their obscure questioning. Oxford and Cambridge universities still occasionally verge on the eccentric when it comes to interviewing prospective graduates. 'If I painted a picture on the side of your house, who would own it?' Exactly.

The point of such questions is to give an insight into how an interviewee forms opinions and constructs an argument about things they have never considered. That's why Cambridge University suggest that over-rehearsing for such questions is a bad idea. They prefer the more spontaneous answers.

It is the same with job interviews. Many companies are equally fond of the bizarre line of questioning, for the same reasons.

In the midst of an interview, you might be asked one of these:

- Why are manhole covers round?
- How do you make M&Ms?
- Is a Jaffa cake a cake or a biscuit?
- How many cans of cat food are sold in America every day?
- If you could be an animal other than a human being, what would you be and why?
- If a spaceship landed outside right now, would you get in it and where would you ask it to take you?

If you are, remember to take the question calmly. You could, of course, decide to get your own back, by asking a surreal question in return when the interviewer delivers that interview standard: 'Have you anything you would like to ask me?'

10.   What is the world's most dangerous job?

If you have to work – and most of us do – surely it is a good idea to do a safe job: one where you can hope to return home at night with all your bones intact, where you don't spend the day in anxious anticipation, other than fear of the occasional amble-by from the boss.

Yet some prefer risk and adventure, working on the edge. For those with an as-yet-unrequited love of danger, forget the relative safety of insurance, banking and other harmless staples of the career officer's suggestions list, and instead consider a few of the following.

There are a lot of dangerous jobs. Lumberjacks have the occasional tree fall on them; aircraft pilots, particularly the light aircraft kind, if unlucky may suffer from 'controlled flight into terrain' (that's flying into the side of a mountain, to the layman); structural iron and steel workers; bomb squad technicians; deep sea divers ... all fairly hazardous.

For sheer unrequited danger, however, nothing beats the lure of the sea and commercial fishing. Imagine: the vastness of the oceans, the moody skies, the freedom of working outdoors, the salty air, the camaraderie of the boat. Try to forget that you are hundreds of miles from anywhere, in stormy seas, working seven-day weeks, 40 out of every 50 hours, in freezing temperatures, when often the ice is so thick on the boat that it can capsize it.

The general consensus, backed up by US and UK statistics, is that the fishing industry is the most dangerous industry in the world to work in.

Just remember that, next time you stub your toe on the office furniture.

11.   Are you in the wrong place or are you the wrong Guy?

Bob Watts is a prosthetist. Not just any kind of prosthetist, but a very good one indeed. He makes artificial limbs for everyone from war veterans to athletes, from toddlers to celebrities such as Heather Mills-McCartney. Did he always want to be doing such worthy work? Not really – it was all a bit of an accident.

As a young man, Bob Watts was in the market for a new job. Having tried a couple of different things he was browsing the job section of the newspaper, looking for an interesting challenge, when he spotted an advert looking for people to make 'artificial arms'.

'That's interesting,' he thought. 'I like children; making toy guns for them could be good fun.'

While the multibillion toy industry has marched on without Bob, he has become one of the world's leading authorities on the manufacture of artificial arms *and* legs.

Sometimes it's the interviewer who gets it wrong. In 2006, a producer for BBC News 24 went down to collect an IT expert due to appear on the show to comment on the Apple v Apple court case.

Guy Goma, a graduate from the Congo, was subsequently taken from the reception area at the BBC studios and straight onto the set for News 24, wired for sound and sat down in the seat to be interviewed live in front of a global TV audience. Unfortunately for Goma, he wasn't an IT expert; he was there for a job interview.

The presenter, Karen Bowerman, asked three questions, which Goma assumed were part of the interview. It made great television for the viewers, but was not so much fun for Goma, who afterwards said that his appearance was 'very brief and very stressful'. Goma didn't get the job, either.

The mix-up happened when the producer went to pick up Guy Kewney, the editor of ewswireless.net, who was later discovered still waiting to be called to the studio. Unfortunately, the producer had not only gone to the wrong reception area, but had also picked up the wrong Guy.

12.   What makes an organisation a great place to work?

Is your organisation a great place to work? Do you get out of bed most mornings looking forward to the day ahead? Or are you filled with dread? If it's the latter, photocopy this page and give it to your boss.

If a company's employees are one of its most important assets (something companies are fond of telling us) then it makes sense to ensure that those employees enjoy turning up for work. It is a little worrying then that, in global consulting firm BlessingWhite's 2006 Employee Engagement Report, while 69 per cent of employees were proud of their organisation, only 18 per cent were fully engaged in their work.

Fortunately for the disengaged masses, some people have been busy researching exactly what organisations need to do to keep their employees 'engaged'.

Employee engagement – a comparatively new HR buzzword – means the level to which people are involved with their organisation. An employee who is engaged in the workplace is willing to go that extra mile, put in more hours, work harder and do what it takes to make the company a success.

Disengaged employees, on the other hand, are not really interested in the success of the company: they work to get through the day, take the money and go home. They don't buy into the values of the company, and are probably job hunting.

There are various rankings of organisations based on employee engagement. Workplace engagement specialist, Best Companies, who compile the UK 'Best Companies to Work For' list for *The Sunday Times*, has surveyed 250,000 people in the UK workforce, in over 1000 different organisations, and produced a list of eight factors with the most bearing on employee engagement.

The top three are:
- *leadership* – how people feel about the head of their organisation, the senior management team and organisational values;
- *well-being* – stress, pressure, the balance between work and home life and the impact of these factors on personal health and performance; and
- *management* – whether people feel supported, trusted and cared for by their immediate manager.

The other factors are: team relationships; the connection between the individual and the organisation; whether a person believes there are opportunities for personal growth; whether employees believe they are getting a fair deal on pay and benefits compared to similar organisations; and how much employees believe the organisation is giving back to society (and the motives for doing so).

A great place to work for, it seems, is not about the occasional balloon trip, day out at the races, champagne breakfast or office party. It is about delivering on those important engagement factors. Not that we are knocking balloon trips or office parties.

13.   Have you got staying power?

You may feel that you are destined for greatness, but somehow you have lost your way. Don't worry: your first step on the career journey is probably not going to be your dream job. There are plenty of people who have carved out a successful business career after a few false starts.

Michael Dell, founder and chairman of Dell Computers, washed dishes in a Chinese restaurant, earning $2.30 an hour; Bill Gates was a congressional page at the Washington state Capitol; Michael Eisner, former CEO of Walt Disney, was a camp counsellor paid $100 (slightly less than the $1 million salary he would earn later in his career); and finally, Madeleine Albright, US Secretary of State from 1997 to 2001, worked in Jocelyn's Department Store in Denver, selling bras.

Others who have steered an erratic course to corporate stardom include Thomas J. Watson, founder of IBM. Watson's first job was as a bookkeeper. He then drove a horse and cart around his neighbourhood selling pianos and sewing machines to farmers.

Hugh Hefner left university and joined the Chicago Cartoon Company in 1949 as an assistant personnel manager. The following year, he took a job as an advertising copywriter for a department store. Then, in his third job in as many years, he began working for *Esquire* magazine as promotion copywriter. It wasn't until *Esquire* announced plans to move to New York that Hefner decided to stay in Chicago and start his own magazine –*Playboy*.

Some people do hit the career jackpot first time out, though. Take a couple of Stanford University students who managed to do just that. From their makeshift research lab – the college dormitory – they developed a new internet search engine and called it BackRub. Then decided to pursue their new business idea rather than college, and changed the name of their idea to ... Google. The duo: Larry Page and Sergey Brin.

14.   Do you have network *nous*?

Knowledge of finance, marketing, operations, logistics, IT and various other business disciplines may play an important part in carving out a successful business career, but don't underestimate the power of networking. Throughout history, business leaders have built empires and fashioned careers through the careful cultivation of contacts.

Take the example of Lord Beaverbrook, one of the 20th century's most successful media magnates. In 1910, Lord Beaverbrook arrived in England from Canada as plain William Maxwell Aitken, a successful businessman looking to make his way in a new country. Using his formidable networking skills, Aitken became a Member of Parliament the year he arrived. Within a short time, his network of contacts included three future Prime Ministers in Lloyd George, Andrew Bonar Law and Winston Churchill. He became Lord Beaverbrook in 1917.

In more modern times, Scott McNealy, the founder of tech giant Sun Micro-systems, engaged in some high-profile networking when he challenged Jack Welch, General Electric's legendary former CEO, to a round of golf. McNealy lost, but so impressed Welch that he received a place on the GE board.

Despite its importance, however, many people find it difficult to get to grips with networking. But as Mary Spillane, author of *Branding Yourself: How to Look, Sound and Behave Your Way to Success*, notes: 'There are people who think it is just getting involved in politics, showing off, schmoozing, a hard sell, but it is anything but that. Networking is about building relationships, because that is what business is about.'

Spillane believes that networking is a skill that can be taught and improved, and, although there is no substitute for practice, Spillane offers, some pointers.

Watch out for bad attitudes, she advises. Don't appear to be out for a hard sell, or just interested in what you want. Tune into the interests and needs of others. Help others before you ask for their help. Don't hand out business cards when no one has asked for them. Don't stick with your own friends when you are in a networking environment. Learn how to do small talk.

15.   Should you get a mentor?

David Pottruck, co-CEO of Charles Schwab & Co., has one. Sir John Browne, former CEO of BP, has had several. Call them CEO coaches, call them mentors, call them what you like. Having someone who is on your side, who understands the world you work in and who has your career's best interests at heart, can make a big difference.

If it's good enough for them, it should be good enough for you. Depending on the kind of relationship you are looking for, and your potential mentor is willing to enter into, a mentor can take on a variety of roles.

A 'counsellor' mentor can help with personal problems. They can advise on the struggle to maintain a work-life balance, and on ethical issues like maintaining personal integrity and values.

A 'coaching' mentor keeps you going when you have trouble motivating yourself. Plus they help you develop skills and techniques to fulfil your goals. They can suggest appropriate strategies for completing tasks as well as providing critical feedback.

Finally, a 'supporter' mentor can be particularly useful for risk-averse people, challenging you to better yourself. With the help of supportive mentoring, providing unconditional support and encouragement, you can take more risks and push yourself beyond your normal boundaries.

How do you actually find your mentor? Quite often you won't need to: they will find you. Failing this, however, it is up to you to identify and approach potential mentors. Talk to your friends and family: they will help you get a better idea of what you are looking for, but may also know someone suitable. Your company may also run a formal mentoring programme so it is worth asking the HR department.

You will need to find someone who is capable of non-judgemental listening and you will have to be open, honest and willing to learn. If you can't do this, you won't be an attractive person to mentor. Both of you will need to be committed to the relationship and find it mutually rewarding.

As Benjamin Disraeli once said: 'The greatest good you can do for another is not just to share your riches, but to reveal to him his own.'

16.   Are you afraid of your job?

Panic attacks in the office? Overcome by dizziness and nausea at the thought of putting in a 9-to-5? Reduced to a shaking jelly of a person by the prospect of some hard graft? Help is at hand. You may be suffering from a legitimate medical condition – ergophobia.

Ergophobia, is not fear of ergs, but, as those of you who can speak Greek will have gathered, fear of work. No, we are not making this up, nor are we making light of the condition. This is not fear of backstabbing colleagues, vending ma-chine coffee or leaky biros; this is full-on, medical-condition-grade fear of work. The kind of fear that, as you might imagine, ruins people's lives.

Some experts believe that phobias are the result of mental conditioning in response to certain situations, and that individuals can be desensitised and cured of their phobias by controlled exposure to the trigger of the phobic response.

With this in mind, for the purposes of sensitisation, we suggest the follow-ing occupations:

- For cheimaphobia*: Worker, Ben & Jerry's spiral hardener conveyor at the Waterbury ice cream factory in Vermont, US. It chills 13,000 pints of ice cream an hour: without the fans off, it's -35; with them on it's -55.
- For linonophobia: Curator, world's largest ball of twine (rolled by a single man) exhibit, Darwin, Minnesota, USA.
- For venustraphobia: Model agency booker, fashion photographer or Miss World judge.

- For batophobia: Mongkok street sweeper, Hong Kong.
- For gamophobia: Wedding official, Little White Wedding Chapel, Las Vegas, Nevada, US (Performed 700 wedding ceremonies on 7/7/2007. Otherwise 100 a day).

[*fear of: cold; string; beautiful women; tall buildings; marriage.]

Section 2: Getting the job done

- Are you addicted to your BlackBerry?
- Will you get fired for photocopying your backside at work?
- Why can't you make personal calls at work?
- Is anyone listening to your presentation?
- Do you underestimate the value of what you are offering?
- Is the customer always right?
- Do you have inbox anxiety?
- Do you enjoy your job?
- How do you brainstorm?
- Do you have a PR problem?
- What's in your lunch box?
- How do you have a productive day?
- Will you get to say goodbye?
- What makes a good speech?
- Are targets a good thing?
- How chic is your cubicle?
- Could you be 'dooced'?
- How do you get the best deal?

17.   Are you addicted to your BlackBerry?

When the Canadian company Research in Motion (RIM) first launched the BlackBerry onto the market in 1999, few realised the impact it would have. As social creatures, humans have always craved contact; now, using these small electronic devices, staying in touch has never been so quick, so easy and so addictive.

Among executives, where the BlackBerry quickly became the must-have business accessory, those that became hooked were known as 'CrackBerry Addicts'. Use of the term CrackBerry became so popular that, in November 2006, Webster's dictionary named CrackBerry its new 'Word of the Year'.

Here are some symptoms of CrackBerry addiction.

- *Furtive working*. This is seen among those BlackBerry users who are aware that they have a problem but are still in control enough to limit their home usage to moments when their spouse is not in the room. Tips for furtive working: phase one – turn the device to silent and place in a discrete position where only you can see the red light (for those not yet addicted, a red light flashes when a new email, text or voice message is received); phase two – drink plenty of water, tea or coffee to ensure regular breaks and therefore opportunities to read and reply to your mail.
- *Repetitive thumb strain*. The design of the BlackBerry means that the quickest way to type emails is by using your thumbs.
- *Restless nights*. The lure of the blinking light on the top of your BlackBerry can lead to poor sleep patterns, with the desire to check for incoming messages in the middle of the night too strong for some users. Even turning it

off may not be enough, if you still have it next to your bed. Try putting it in another room altogether

- *Fretful children*. Children that find they have to compete for attention with a new addition to the family may become fretful or downright hostile. Kids have been known to hide BlackBerrys, or even attempt to flush them down the toilet.

18. Will you get fired for photocopying your backside at work?

Under normal conditions, people tend not to place their naked backside on a sheet of glass and sit down. However, at Christmas parties rules may go out of the window.

And, as the dozen or so A3 images of your derrière spill out of the copier, you are probably breaking numerous rules, written or otherwise, so there is every chance that you could be subject to disciplinary procedures. But is the year end/rear end tradition of photocopying your backside as popular as the urban myths would have us believe?

It seems that it is, with Canon, the photocopying machine specialists, reporting a 25 per cent increase in emergency call-outs over Christmas, a large proportion of them to repair shattered glass. Canon even responded by increasing the glass thickness from 4 mm to 5 mm in an effort to reduce the number of occasions when a light-hearted prank turns into a trip to the nearest hospital.

It's not just backsides that end up on or in the photocopier. In 2005, Canon surveyed both their customers and their technicians. It discovered that items recovered from photocopiers included mice, a sleeping cat, spiders, a crab, a swarm of bees, a cockroach, a snake, a kitchen knife, a sausage roll, stockings, dominoes, a cheque for £6000, a vibrator, a condom and, of course, paper jams with rather incriminating evidence on them. One service engineer had repaired a machine which was jammed with images of a man's groin.

19.   Why can't you make personal calls at work?

In March 2007, the Canadian media ran a story about someone making a mobile phone call while driving. Not that unusual. But this was no ordinary driver – it was a bus driver, who, according to the passenger who took the pictures, spent some 30 minutes on what was clearly a personal phone call.

We've all done it. A quick personal call here, a few minutes browsing for your holiday there … maybe you even have your personal instant messaging switched on while you are working. It doesn't take up much time, so how could it be a problem?

Small businesses in the UK spend around £400 million a year on personal calls made by employees on company phones and mobiles, according to research by Aurora Kendrick James, telecom expense specialists.

The top seven ways of wasting company time were:

1   Surfing the internet: 52%
2   Socialising with co-workers: 26.3%
3   Running off-site errands: 7.6%
4   Spacing out: 6.6%
5   Making personal phone calls: 3.9%

6　Arriving late and leaving early: 2.9%

7　Applying for other jobs: 0.7%

In the US, a survey conducted by America Online and Salary.com found that employees keeping on top of their personal life costs companies billions of dollars each year. The average American worker spends 1.86 hours per 8-hour day on non-work-related activities, before adding legitimate breaks and lunch. This equates to an estimated $544 billion worth of time where people should be working yet aren't.

20.　Is anyone listening to your presentation?

In 1957, US Senator Strom Thurmond, rose before the US Senate to speak on the Voting Rights Bill debate. It was about 9.00 am. Thurmond was well prepared, having spent time earlier dehydrating himself in the Senate steam room. He was equipped with a steak sandwich lunch, malted milk tablets, throat lozenges and a vast amount of reading material. For the next 24 hours and 18 minutes, Thurmond proceeded to talk out the bill, a political tactic known as filibustering. In doing so, he began by reading the election statutes for every US state. He then moved on to read and discuss the Declaration of Independence, the Bill of Rights, and Washington's Farewell Address. He only left the floor at the insistence of his staff, who were concerned for his health.

While Thurmond managed to stay awake for the duration, it is unlikely anyone else did. Thurmond wasn't concerned about capturing his audience, and it's a good job too, as he would have had an empty auditorium. For most people who have to give a presentation, however, tedium will not be tolerated. Especially in the so-called graveyard slot when everyone has had their fill of the lunchtime buffet.

Good speakers grab the audience's attention straight away and maintain a vice-like grip on it thereafter. A great example of this was when Martin Luther King delivered his 'I have a dream' speech on the 28 August 1963. He took the audience on a journey that the entire world would never forget. Fortunately, those in the know have passed on some advice on holding an audience.

Practising the speech is essential. Get familiar with the content, but try not to learn it parrot fashion, which can be a disaster if you lose your place. Use bullet points, and break down the sections into time periods, so you can lose a section if necessary.

Confidence is important. You have probably been asked to give the speech because you are the best person for the job. Act like you are, and never apologise for your lack of experience or lack of time to prepare. Also make sure that, when you are introduced, your credibility is established.

Finally, if you want to make sure that the audience doesn't leave early, include plenty of provocative facts or questions, share relevant personal experiences and stories, use analogies and, if appropriate, props, such as visual images.

And try to keep the speech shorter than Senator Thurmond's.

21.   Do you underestimate the value of what you are offering?

Sabeer Bhatia, the founder of web-based email company Hotmail, knows how to negotiate. He could have sold Hotmail to Microsoft for tens of millions.

Microsoft came to the negotiating table with a six-strong team. Bhatia, however, elected to negotiate alone so that he could avoid divide and rule tactics. First, the Microsoft team returned to Bhatia's every fortnight for two months. Then, Bill Gates invited Bhatia to Redmond for a chat.

Bhatia asked for $700 million. Microsoft offered tens of millions. Bhatia said no. Microsoft offered $200 million. Bhatia said no. Microsoft offered $300 million. Bhatia said no. Microsoft offered $350 million. Bhatia's staff at Hotmail quietly suggested he should secure their future by accepting. Bhatia's management team said he should accept. Bhatia said no.

When the deal was done at an undisclosed price, 2,769,148 of Microsoft shares were exchanged for ownership – a value of $400 million at the time of the deal. Some might question whether it was great negotiating, stubbornness or plain foolhardiness.

The key to Bhatia's success was that he knew the value of what he was selling. One of the golden rules of deal-making is 'don't underestimate the value of what you are offering'. It's an easy mistake to make. Especially when there is a lot of money already on the table.

Not everyone possesses Bhatia's innate gift for negotiation. But even the most inept negotiators – the kind who come away from the used-car lot having paid full price for a motor car, but still feeling pleased – can learn to avoid common negotiating pitfalls. In a 2001 *Harvard Business Review* article, 'Six habits of merely effective negotiators', Harvard Business School professor James K. Sebenius, founder of the school's negotiation unit, outlines six negotiation errors: neglecting the other side's problems; letting price get in the way of other interests; letting positions drive out interests; searching too hard for common ground; neglecting the best alternative to a negotiated agreement; and getting too committed to your point of view.

You may not be negotiating for $400 million, but every deal counts.

22.   Is the customer always right?

You would think so, if you gave any credence to the usual customer service mantra. But the bosses of some of the world's most successful companies might disagree.

Gordon Bethune, who turned Continental Airways around, believed in a robust defence of his employees, when necessary. As he says in his book *From Worst To First: Behind the Scenes of Continental's Remarkable Comeback*,

'When it's a choice between supporting your employees, who work with you every day and make your product what it is, or some irate jerk who demands a free ticket to Paris because you ran out of peanuts, whose side are you going to be on? ... if they think that you won't support them when a customer is out of line, even the smallest problem can cause resentment.'

Herb Kelleher, founder and former CEO of Southwest Airlines also believed in sticking up for his employees. In the book *Nuts!*, by Kevin and Jackie Freiberg, which recounts the success of the airline, the authors tell the story of a frequent complainer. This particular woman complained just about every time she flew, whether about the peanuts or the flight attendant's outfits. The airline has a policy of replying to all customer complaints, but at some point one of the lady's letters found its way onto Kelleher's desk. According to the then Director of Customer Relations, Jim Ruppel, and the Director of Corporate Employment, Sherry Phelps, Kelleher wrote back: 'Dear Mrs. Crabapple, We will miss you. Love, Herb.'

Just as customers who complain aren't always right, neither do consumers always know what they want. The trend today is to run consumer focus groups on just about anything new, from advertising to product design. The buzzword is 'co-creation' where the consumer inputs into product development. Yet some of the most innovative and successful products have been conceived and launched on a hunch.

The Sony Walkman was the brainchild of Akio Morita, Sony's visionary leader. Morita noticed that young people liked listening to music regardless of location, so he invented a portable tape cassette player. He then had to convince his sceptical colleagues. Customer focus groups were nowhere to be seen. 'Our plan is to lead the public rather than ask them what products they want. The public does not know what is possible, but we do,' he said.

Morita got his way over the name too, eventually. Sony America thought the name poor English and changed it to Soundabout for the US market. It was known as Freestyle in Sweden, and Stowaway in the UK. As soon as Morita received a bad set of sales figures, he used it as an excuse to change the name to Walkman.

Perhaps companies should trust their instincts more often. As Henry Ford once remarked: 'If I'd asked my customers what they wanted, they'd have said a faster horse.'

23.   Do you have inbox anxiety?

A new kind of bankruptcy made the news in 2006 –email bankruptcy. Venture capitalist Fred Wilson announced in his blog that he was declaring email bankruptcy and abandoning attempts to keep up with a substantial backlog of email. A surge in email bankruptcies ensued.

The term appears to date back to Lawrence Lessig, Professor of Law at Stanford Law School and founder of the school's Centre for Internet and Society. In 2004, Lessig sent an email to a number of people saying: 'Dear person who sent me a yet-unanswered e-mail, I apologise, but I am declaring e-mail bankruptcy.' Lessig had spent 80 hours the week before, sifting through a pile of unanswered e-mail dating back to January 2002. He also apologised for his lack of 'cyber decency'.

There are few people with a work email account who can't empathise with Wilson and Lessig and other email bankrupts. We are, collectively, suffering from email overload.

The statistics vary, but the numbers are universally impressive (or scary, depending on how you look at them). Ferris Research, a San Francisco research firm specialising in messaging and collaborative technologies, estimates that six trillion business emails were sent in 2006.

Research by Professor Deborah Valentine at the Goizueta Business Writing Centre, and Ruth Pagell, the former Executive Director of Goizueta's Centre for Business Information (CBI), found that, of 1200 executives surveyed, over 50 per cent spent at least two hours per day answering email at work and 30 per cent spent an additional hour or more at home. That's about four months per year dealing with emails.

Barring declaring yourself an email bankrupt, how can you cope with the mountain of email stacked up in your inbox? Henley Management Centre carried out a survey on email use on behalf of Plantronics, a UK telecoms equipment company, recently. It concluded that European managers spend at least ten years of their life dealing with email – and offered some useful tips for managing email.

Henley's guidelines included:

- dealing with emails in blocks of time, rather than as they arrive;
- turning off auto-alert;
- not copying the whole of the office in on every email you send – do it on a need-to-know basis;
- not forwarding jokes, video clips, email scams, viral messages and other non-work related and unnecessary emails – and if you do, send them to the person's personal home email address.

24.   Do you enjoy your job?

Research indicates that as many as 87 per cent of Americans don't like their jobs, which, when you estimate the number of hours worked over a lifetime as approximately 90,000, makes pretty depressing reading.

So if we spend that much time working, surely we should be enjoying ourselves. If not, perhaps it is time to start browsing the appointment sections. To help you decide if it's time to knuckle down or move on, here are some things you need to ask:

1   *Why did I start doing this in the first place?* It can be easy to forget why you started to work in a specific industry or job.
2   *Am I only seeing the negative aspects of my job?* Take some time to think about the positive aspects of your job to help give a balanced view.
3   *Would I enjoy my job more if it were more challenging?* Increasing responsibilities and challenges can breathe new life into a stale job.
4   *Can I rejuvenate the motivation and enjoyment I used to have for my job?* If you can't find motivation or enjoyment in what you do, perhaps it is time to move on.

If you decide to head down a new career pathway, you may as well pick one that you enjoy. The 2006 General Social Survey of 27,000 random Americans reported the following jobs that people enjoyed the most:

- Clergy 87%
- Fire fighters 80%
- Physical therapists 78%
- Authors 74%
- Special education teachers 70%
- Teachers 69%
- Education administrators 68%
- Painters and sculptors 67%
- Psychologists 67%
- Security and financial services salespeople 65%
- Operating engineers 64%
- Office supervisors 61%

25.   How do you brainstorm?

Brainstorming may be an activity dismissed by the more rationally minded, who like to be able to measure input, output and performance. However, there is no question that sitting around firing out ideas has been very important to the performance of many organisations. Nokia, the mobile phone company, had its fortunes transformed by a new CEO, Jorma Ollila, with the help of brainstorming sessions.

In 1992, Ollila emerged from a brainstorming meeting with a new, compelling vision of the future for his company: 'Telecom-oriented, global focus, value-added.' He then spent the next few years driving these words down through the once-unwieldy, old-fashioned conglomerate, to create today's world beating corporate star. Brainstorming plays an integral part in Nokia's strategy development.

Invention of the term 'brainstorming' is attributed to advertising executive Alex Osborn, of ad agency BDO, who wrote about the technique in his book *Your Creative Power*, published in 1948. It is not know whether the term was the product of a brainstorming session.

Many companies place brainstorming at the heart of the innovation that drives their organisation. International design firm IDEO was once described by *Fortune* magazine as 'one of Silicon Valley's secret weapons', an organisation that has produced such diverse projects as helping create the very first Apple computer mouse and the design of the 25-foot mechanical whale in the *Free Willy* films.

The company adopts a special approach to brainstorming. Project leaders call a brainstorming session at the start of a new assignment, inviting particular people to attend. Most sessions involve a multi-disciplinary group of around eight participants.

When the brainstorming starts, creativity is given free rein. Participants can doodle or scribble on almost anything: there are whiteboards on the walls, and conference tables covered in white paper, plus high-tech multimedia presentations.

The firm has written down its five principles of brainstorming: stay focused on the topic; encourage wild ideas; defer judgement; build on the ideas of others; and one conversation at a time. For information on how not to brainstorm, see *The Incredible Adventures of Professor Branestawm* by Norman Hunter.

26.   Do you have a PR problem?

In 2007, Cadbury Schweppes launched a treasure hunt across 23 American cities in a promotional campaign that promised up to £760,000 to anyone who found one of its hidden gold coins. Unfortunately the agency hired to bury a coin in Boston, Massachusetts, chose the 347-year-old Granary Burying Ground.

When anxious officials realised what was going on they were forced to close the cemetery before any of the graves were desecrated. In turn, Cadbury Schweppes had to move quickly to avert a publicity disaster, apologising to the authorities.

Irish author dramatist Brendan Behan may have asserted that 'there is no such thing as bad publicity, except your own obituary,' but events in the corporate world appear to contradict his view. It is unlikely that Virgin Trains rejoice every time the media runs a story like that in November 2006, of passengers on a Virgin Pendolino train being asked if they had any nuts and bolts on them to help fix a faulty windscreen wiper.

As Virgin and Branson know only too well, publicity can be a very important marketing weapon and brand-building tool, if used in the right way. Hence Branson's many forays into the public arena wearing all manner of outfits – a wedding dress, a pilot's outfit, a space suit – to publicise various Virgin ventures, and with remarkable success. Yet publicity is a double-edged sword, and has to be handled very carefully, as the adverse publicity surrounding Virgin's rail activities demonstrates. Unfortunately, justified or otherwise, mud sticks.

Many people court publicity on a regular basis, and many have advisors to help them negotiate the perils. For those who don't but who decide to drum up some publicity anyway, just remember that ill thought-out or badly delivered publicity can have dire consequences.

Heed the salutary tale of Gerald Ratner, who was the head of Ratners, a leading chain of retail jewellers in the UK. In 1991, he made a speech to an audience at the Institute of Directors, during which he made some injudicious comments about the company's £4.99 sherry decanter set, proclaiming it to be 'total crap'. He propounded his mistake by telling his audience that Ratners sold a pair of earrings for under £1, which was cheaper than a prawn sandwich from Marks & Spencer, but, added Ratner, probably wouldn't last as long.

Ratner got a big laugh from the audience but at the expense of unwanted media publicity about his remarks, which dented consumer confidence in the firm's products, and was estimated to have knocked £500m from the value of the company.

27.   What's in your lunch box?

The notion that eating specific things will help you through your day is not a new one. It's common sense, after all. But what is considered to be a healthy choice changes regularly.

The famous 1960's 'Go to Work on an Egg' advertising campaign, starring comedian Tony Hancock, extolled the virtues, as you would expect, of eggs. However, when the British Egg Information Service (BEIS) wanted to rerun the television adverts in 2007, they were blocked by a government-backed watch-

dog on the grounds that eating an egg for breakfast every day does not consti-
tute a healthy and varied diet.

Unfortunately, this advice came too late for Paul Newman who, in his 1967
film *Cool Hand Luke*, attempted to eat 50 hard-boiled eggs in an hour. He didn't
look too perky by the end of it.

So what should we eat? Experts say that, if you want to sail through the day
with energy to spare, a healthy diet should derive 50 per cent of the energy you
require from carbohydrates, 30 per cent from fat and 20 per cent from protein.

Everyone needs to eat as wide a variety of foods as possible to ensure they
are getting enough vitamins and minerals. No one food contains all of the vitamins and minerals we need, therefore the wider the variety, the more likely it
is that people will get all the nutrients required. Eating foods with fibre helps
to slow the digestion process and so provide energy release over a sustained
period of time. You should also be drinking around two litres of water a day.

Spreading your food intake as evenly as possible throughout the day provides a more sustained energy release, helping to keep the metabolism up and
utilising vitamins efficiently. As for how much you should consume, we suggest
you eat until you're 'hara hachi bu' – this phrase, which comes from the Japanese island Okinawa, means 'eat only until you are 80 per cent full' and is a
great guide for controlling your calorie intake. The Okinawans know a thing or
two about healthy living too. After all, they live longer than any other group of
people. The average life expectancy on Okinawa is 85 years, and they have more
centenarians there than anywhere else in the world.

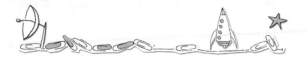

28.   How do you have a productive day?

Gone are the days of the Stakhanovite miners, named after a hero of the Soviet Union, Alexey Grigoryevich Stakhanov. Stakhanov was famed for his incredible productivity after, in August 1935, he reportedly mined a record 102 tons of coal in 5 hours and 45 minutes – a staggering 14 times his quota. In the following month he was said to have mined 227 tons in a single shift.

Stakhanov's records were hailed as an example for everyone throughout the Soviet Union as the state tried to encourage workers to exceed production targets. An additional measure intended to sharpen the focus of the workforce was the promise of periods of time in the Corrective Labour Camps and Colonies, otherwise known as the Gulags, for those who failed to meet their quotas.

You may not be as productive as Stakhanov, and hopefully you will not be threatened with the Gulags, but there is much you can do to improve your personal productivity. Great entrepreneurs do it naturally; corporate hotshots have ultra-efficient personal assistants to help them do it. But no matter who you are, the key to being productive is managing the use of your time.

If Stakhanov was still alive he might have suggested the following:

- Have a 'to do' list in the form of a breakdown of tasks that you have to achieve. This will help you focus on what needs to be done. Write it out at the beginning of the week and include personal as well as work-related tasks. It's also worth remembering that having a 'to do' list is useless if you don't do the most important things first.

- Put everything into your diary and allocate enough time. Keeping careful track of your commitments will give you confidence that you are on top of everything. Also avoid the temptation of multi-tasking if at all possible. This may work for some tasks, but for more complex things, multi-tasking makes you less productive as it takes time to get back up to speed.
- Finally, it is worth looking at some research conducted by Lexmark. In its survey, Lexmark discovered that British workers may put in long hours at the office but they are also the most distracted. The average British worker wastes 22 per cent of the working day making tea, gossiping and planning for their next holiday.

The likelihood is that, if the only holiday destination available to them was a working holiday in the Gulags, this percentage would drop considerably.

29.   Will you get to say goodbye?

There was a time when the worst a disgruntled employee would do was to steal a few pencils or badmouth their work colleagues. Today, however, one person can undo years of work and cost a business a small fortune, all with the click of a mouse. Many companies are, therefore, adopting a policy of whisking people out of the office as fast as they can.

Newspaper editors have long been familiar with the long march to the door, without the opportunity to clear their desk. When Piers Morgan was sacked as editor of the *Daily Mirror* in 2004, he was relieved of his electronic pass providing access to the paper's offices, and physically escorted off the premises. It all happened so quickly that he didn't have time to collect his jacket and mobile phone, which were brought down to him later by his secretary. He joins a long line of illustrious editors who have exited their offices in a similarly brisk manner.

It may all seem a little excessive, but companies do have cause for concern. Some disgruntled employees have wreaked havoc on their former employers. When peeved network engineer, Timothy Lloyd, remotely triggered a software 'bomb' following his dismissal from Omega Engineering, he cost the business an estimated $10 million. The software bomb went off in the central file server, which housed more than 1000 programmes; it erased and purged everything. The company, which made high-tech equipment for the Navy and NASA, was crippled. Lloyd was eventually sentenced to 41 months in prison.

30.   What makes a good speech?

If you are inching your way up the greasy pole of success, the likelihood is that you will have to make a speech or presentation at some time.

You may not stir a nation with the words you utter, like the great orator Winston Churchill so often did. Your delivery may not become as famous as the Gettysburg Address that Abraham Lincoln gave in 1863. But, if you want to keep your job and pay those bills, it had better be at least half-decent.

Making a good speech is about the relevance it has at the moment in time when it is delivered. When Charles Spencer, brother of the late Princess Diana, spoke at his sister's funeral, the whole world was watching and listening. He delivered a spellbinding tirade against the media, accusing them of turning Diana into 'the most hunted person of the modern age'. As he said later: 'It poured out from the heart, not the head.'

Delivering a coherent speech from the heart is a skill that only few can master. It is especially difficult when referring to something that is pre-planned and written.

Experts suggest that thorough preparation of content is the key to success. The following 'do's and 'don't's will help you determine if the content you have is correct.

Do

- Determine what the focus of your presentation is
- Know what the audience's knowledge is
- Have a powerful start
- Establish your credibility
- Include some element of education
- Define jargon
- Create an ebb and flow
- Use stories
- Use appropriate humour.

Don't

- Fill your PowerPoint slides with exactly the words you intend to speak
- Have an excessive number of facts – they won't be remembered
- Finish abruptly without summarising your presentation
- Patronise.

31.   Are targets a good thing?

There are few jobs that exist where there isn't some sort of target attached to performance, which in turn impacts on the objectives of the organisation. That target may well be tied to the pay and benefits of the individual concerned.

The problem is that, while target setting is almost universally accepted as a beneficial, if occasionally unpalatable, thing, there is some very robust research suggesting that target setting can be a very destructive force within an organisation.

Of course, there are many examples where the use of targets has produced an excellent outcome for those involved. However, there are numerous instances where targets have failed, where people have cheated and twisted the system to hit targets and, in some cases, left an organisation in a worse situation.

In Scotland, GPs were set a target of seeing every patient who requested a doctor's appointment within 48 hours. How did practices choose to meet this worthy target? By restricting their systems so patients could only book appointments for the same day that they phoned their GP surgery. This caused patients who needed regular check-ups to call back day after day, jamming phone lines, as they tried to secure an appointment. Target met, but quality of service reduced.

This kind of behaviour shouldn't be unexpected, as it is predicted by Maurice Schweitzer, Professor of Operations and Information Management at Wharton, University of Pennsylvania, one of the world's leading business schools.

In 'Goal Setting as a Motivator of Unethical Behaviour' published in *The Academy of Management Journal*, Schweitzer explains that goal setting has a dark side to it. In addition to motivating constructive behaviour, goal setting – especially when it involves rewards – can motivate unethical behaviour when people fall short of the goals they set or that are set for them. This is particularly true when people fall just short of their targets.

Schweitzer points to the spate of business scandals in recent years. Executives get caught cooking the books to meet quarterly goals demanded by Wall Street analysts. Salesmen report fake sales, or exaggerate them. Manufacturers ship unfinished products. Much of this behaviour is because of the need to hit internal or external sales targets.

In their research, Schweitzer and his co-authors found that 'people with unmet goals were more likely to engage in unethical behaviour than people attempting to do their best.' Thought-provoking findings given the target driven culture we live in.

32.   How chic is your cubicle?

In the book *Future Shock*, published in 1970, Alvin Toffler, one of the world's leading futurists, predicted a world where society 'shifts from a work orientation towards greater involvement in leisure.' Toffler wasn't alone in his optimistic view of the 21st century and beyond. There was considerable agreement that technological advances would create increased productivity and increased leisure-time. In the developed economies at least, a post-industrial leisure based society awaited.

Unfortunately, the age of leisure has failed to materialise. Quite the opposite has happened. Most of us work longer hours than ever. As it became apparent that the Utopian vision of an idyllic world without work was misplaced, attention turned to how the workplace, and our workspace, might evolve instead, making our working lives more efficient and more pleasant.

There were many bold predictions. Workers would be liberated from the confines of the office by technologies such as the laptop, wi-fi broadband, the internet, email, voice over internet protocol, instant messaging and cell phones. Armies of executives would travel the globe as mobile human offices, connected to their colleagues and customers by modern technology. Yet, while the road warrior does exist, many workers are still firmly entrenched in a physical workspace – the office.

Nor does that workspace look like the futuristic predictions of the Harvard Graduate School of Design, where they are creating design guidelines for new convergent business architecture. The aim is to seamlessly merge the physical and virtual worlds. Other anticipated changes such as hot desking or hotelling (sharing a desk, workstation or other resource normally allocated to one person), huddle spaces and touchdown areas (informal meeting areas designed to foment creativity and personal communication) are slowly seeping into organisational consciousness.

For the masses, the reality is the cubicle. According to *Fortune* magazine, forty million Americans work in cubicles. There's even a 'how to spruce up your cubicle' book, *Cube Chic*. If you are looking for someone to blame, Robert Propst is the name you are after. In 1968, Herman Miller, a home furnishings firm in the US, launched a new concept in office furnishings – the Action Office. It was the forerunner of the modern cubicle. Although Propst, the firm's president and chief inventor, didn't envisage his brainchild quite that way, sadly, economics plus Action Office equals hundreds of tiny cubicles crammed onto the office floor.

33.   Could you be 'dooced'?

Blogging is mainstream. There are some 86 million blogs – web logs – and rising, apparently. Even senior executives are getting in on the act. Now anyone and everyone can discover the innermost thoughts, hopes and fears of the great and good of business ... or some of them at least.

At the last count, a quick Google search revealed that General Motors – yes, that traditional non high-tech auto industry company – has a blog, posted by tech-savvy septuagenarian vice chairman Bob Lutz. Joseph B. Wikert, a Vice President at publishing outfit Wiley, has Joe Wikert's Publishing 2020 blog. Not to forget the inside-the-company view from Sun Microsystems' President and COO, Jonathan Schwartz.

A note of caution though, for those who are about to join, or already are, part of the blogging community. According to the 2006 Workplace E-Mail, Instant Messaging & Blog Survey from American Management Association (AMA) and the ePolicy Institute, nearly 2 per cent of companies surveyed had fired workers – that's 'dooced', in blogger language – for posting offensive blog content, including posts on employees' personal home-based blogs.

The risks associated with blogging include defamation, copyright infringement, trade secret theft, and various other legal and privacy issues. Only 9 per cent of organisations had policies in place to cover business blogging; and only 7 per cent had rules governing the content posted by employees on their home-based personal blogs.

A famous victim of blogging fallout is Ellen Simonetti, a former flight attendant in the US who worked for Delta Airlines. Simonetti posted pictures of herself in her work uniform on her blog *Queen of Sky: Diary of a Dysfunctional Flight Attendant*. The snaps were deemed inappropriate by her employers. You can check out the pics on her retitled blog – *Queen of Sky: Diary of a Fired Flight Attendant*.

34.   How do you get the best deal?

Negotiating is an important skill, both in life generally and in work specifically. Like playing poker, part of negotiating is about knowing, or at least judging, whether the person you are dealing with is telling the truth or bluffing (some might call that lying). If you can tell when someone is being economical with the truth, it gives you an important advantage.

Most people would like to think they can tell when someone's lying. The telltale signs are well publicised and an obvious giveaway: fidgeting, refusing to make eye contact, blinking nervously, a shifty demeanour, stroking the back of the head or scratching the nose.

But research suggests that it is not as easy as that. Studies by Dr Samantha Mann, a psychologist at Portsmouth University, show that, rather than fidget and look shifty, liars tend to be thinking harder and, as a result, moving less. Self-adaptor gestures – touching the hair and face, for example – are less common with liars. And so is pointing.

There are some giveaway signs, however. Metaphoric gestures – holds hands apart to show size, as in 'the fish was this big' – are 25 per cent more common with liars. Emblematic gestures – body movements that convey specific messages, such as the thumbs up, to indicate everything is OK – are also slightly more common with liars, as is the rhythmic gesture –jabbing fingers into the air, for example.

Other research that Mann carried out included studying the behaviour of suspects during police interviews. Mann discovered that the suspects who lied blinked less than the truthful suspects; they also paused more often while speaking. Eighty one per cent of suspects paused longer or blinked less when telling fibs.

So next time you are negotiating a deal, and the person you are negotiating with tells you that these are the very best terms they can offer – while pausing frequently, looking you in the eye without blinking, and occasionally jabbing the air – it's safe to assume that there is still some negotiating to be done.

Section 3: Working with others

- What is the best way to fire someone?
- How do you deal with sponsoring everyone at work?
- Do you know Kevin Bacon?
- Is your employer watching you?
- Why do people always gather around the water cooler?
- Can you be friends with your team?
- Can you beat the bully?
- Are you assertive?
- Are you a control freak?
- Is it ok to sleep on the job?
- Are you emotionally intelligent?
- Are you actively listening?
- Does your team need a leader?
- Are you working with Edward Deadwood?
- How big does your network need to be?
- Are you having a laugh?
- Can you smooch in the storeroom?

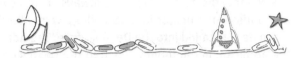

35.   What is the best way to fire someone?

'You're fired' – it's a phrase that workers are less familiar with these days, unless they are keen viewers of *The Apprentice*, that is. That's not because people don't get fired. It is just that the days when the boss called an errant employer into their office, shut the door, much to the consternation of the rest of the office, and then duly fired them face-to-face, using straightforward language, seem to be growing fewer.

Now, with the advent of electronic high-tech communications and the impersonal society we live in, a boss can fire someone from the other side of the globe.

In 2006, RadioShack in the US received some adverse publicity when it fired 400 employees by email. Part of the email text read: 'The workforce reduction notification is currently in progress. Unfortunately, your position is one that has been eliminated.'

Whether it is because of rightsizing, realignment, reengineering, downsizing or restructuring, displacement by email is likely to increase. In fact, if there is technology available, employers will use it. These days people get sacked by voicemail, email, video conferencing … even text message.

Take the case of the Accident Group, the UK-based personal injury claims company. One Friday in May 2003, many of the company's employees received a text message informing them that they were being made redundant.

Not that the personal touch is always an improvement. One person working as Admissions Director in a US college was interviewing a potential student when he was called into the Dean's office. The Admissions Director, having left the applicant mid-interview, went to the Dean's office whereupon he was told that he was being replaced by a computer system.

36. How do you deal with sponsoring everyone at work?

Dave is going trekking again in a far-flung location, which sounds like a holiday but will actually raise money for a donkey sanctuary. Joan is doing a knit-athon to help the local hospice, and for an extra £10 you will get one of the many scarves she intends to create. Sally from accounts is going to walk what sounds like an incredibly long way, especially as she intends to wear little more than her underwear. She has even brought the bra into the office for you to see.

Every one of their efforts is for a worthy cause, but it can feel as though the world of charity is taking a big bite out of your monthly pay cheque. Peer pressure is every bit as prevalent in the workplace as it was at school. Pleasing others while still trying to please yourself can be tricky, and charitable giving is an area that can produce such a dilemma.

Figures in UK Giving 2005/06 showed that the UK adult population gave a total of £8.9 billion, with an average donation of £15.28 per person per month. It is estimated that 57.6 per cent of the population give to charity in an average month.

Of course, you could join the 42.4 per cent who choose not to give, but there are many who simply feel obliged or don't want to run the risk of being ostracised. So if you are going to give, try to do it efficiently.

Gift Aid is the best choice. It allows a charity to reclaim the basic-rate tax on donations made by UK taxpayers from the Inland Revenue. In addition, higher-rate taxpayers can claim 18 per cent tax relief on the gross amount of their donation, meaning that the donation costs them less.

This way, even if Joan develops a repetitive strain injury, prematurely bringing her knitting days to an end, you can still feel that the value of your philanthropic gesture was maximised.

37.   Do you know Kevin Bacon?

Yes, the actor. You may not know him personally, but you probably know someone who does, or at least know someone who knows someone, who knows someone, who knows someone, who knows someone, who knows Kevin Bacon.

This is the concept of 'six degrees of separation', a term popularised by American playwright, John Guare in the play of the same name. In the play, written in 1990, and adapted as a film starring Will Smith in 1993, one of the characters philosophises about the fact that any two people, even the US President and a gondolier in Venice, are separated by only five other people.

As is usual with these ideas, various people are attributed with its conception. Some dated the concept back to Marconi, who suggested that on average any two people are 5.83 people apart. Later, in the 1960s, Harvard social psychologist Stanley Milgram undertook some research that showed it took an average of six steps for a letter sent to a random resident of Omaha, Nebraska to be sent on to a target person in Boston – using only each person's contacts to form the chain.

Following Guare's play, the idea of six degrees was popularised via the internet and the 'Six degrees of Kevin Bacon' puzzle. For those who don't know, Kevin Bacon is a successful Hollywood actor who has starred in, among others, that celluloid classic, *Tremors*. The aim is to link Kevin Bacon with any other actor using only six (or seven) connected steps.

So, for example, how is Carrie Fisher connected to Kevin Bacon? Carrie Fisher was in *Star Wars* with Harrison Ford who was in *The Fugitive* with Tommy Lee Jones who was in *Batman Forever* with Val Kilmer who was in *Heat* with Robert DeNiro who was in *Sleepers* with Kevin Bacon.

Bacon appears to have taken the game in good spirit. In January 2007, he launched SixDegrees.org, a charitable social network created in partnership with the non-profit Network for Good, AOL, and *Entertainment Weekly*.

While knowing Kevin Bacon through six degrees of separation may not improve your career prospects much, the concept just serves to illustrate what is known as the small world phenomenon. The likelihood is that you know someone, who knows someone, etc., who might improve your career prospects. Now all you have to do is work out who they are.

38.   Is your employer watching you?

They may not be watching you right this minute. But they may well be reading your emails, tracking your surfing habits, and eavesdropping on your calls. Employers can even track employee's movements via GPS, both during and after working hours. This has already happened in the US.

The figures suggest that employee surveillance is commonplace. One survey, for example, revealed that 92 per cent of employers monitored employees' e-mail; 76 per cent monitored internet use; and 22 per cent taped phone conversations.

Electronic surveillance of all types is widespread. It includes smart cards, biometric data, computers that log keystrokes and web and email usage, telephone bugging, video surveillance and bar codes. In addition to this, there is drug, medical and genetic testing.

In the UK, the Trades Union Congress drew up a *Stop Snooping* report, which referred to research in the US that demonstrated that employees who are monitored (and presumably are aware of that monitoring) suffered greater depression, dissatisfaction with work, exhaustion, and anxiety than unmonitored workers. They were also more likely to suffer neck problems.

Presumably from constantly looking over their shoulder.

39.   Why do people always gather around the water cooler?

The water cooler, photocopier and coffee-making machine are all places where employees interact in the workplace; where, as well as idle chitchat and gossip, important ideas and information are exchanged. But have you ever wondered what the attraction is?

Plenty of companies have. No wonder that, in an age where creativity and knowledge sharing are supposed to be at the heart of organisational competitiveness, companies have tried to bottle the essence of that magical water cooler interaction and sprinkle it throughout the organisation.

Open-plan offices, for example, were introduced by many companies in the 1980s to encourage spontaneous interaction. Some companies went even further. Scandinavian Air Systems (SAS) transformed part of the company's headquarters into a street scene, complete with shops and meeting spaces, but it appeared to have little discernible effect on employee behaviour, or at least in the way that they might have hoped.

Fortunately for organisational heads and lovers of informal conversation, two business school academics – John Weeks, an assistant professor at INSEAD, the international business school based in France, and Anne-Laure Fayard, an assistant professor at Polytechnic University, Brooklyn, New York – have deconstructed the water cooler or photocopier moment to bring us the rules of engagement. They did this by videoing people's behaviour in the photocopy room, and discovered three essential factors for informal exchange of information and ideas.

The first factor was privacy – a soundproofed room, for example, puts people at their ease. The second factor was propinquity * – the opportunity to socialise, but in a way that makes interaction take place. It is the difference between travelling in a lift with someone and being trapped in a lift with them. Finally came social designation, which is about how a space makes people feel. Bright lights and spartan rooms are not conducive to conversation, which is why modern bars have low lighting and comfy seating.

Manufacturing the water cooler moment requires all three factors. Despite SAS's ingenious efforts, using a high street concept that connected eating, shopping, sports facilities and rooms with comfortable furniture for meetings, it lacked privacy. Employees still chose to take meetings in private rooms. It's not easy capturing the magic of that water cooler moment.

*The authors apologise for the occasional long word and tortuous syntax (see back cover copy).

40.   Can you be friends with your team?

In some ways, football management has interesting parallels with the world of business, not least in the area of man management. At the highest level, football managers have to manage a team of highly talented individuals, who are paid very large sums of money, and are used to being treated with great reverence in some quarters. Quite similar to managing a senior executive team, then. One key to success seems to be the ability to assess the needs of the individual team members – how to balance the need to support, empathise and praise – with the need to discipline and maintain order and team spirit, while retaining authority.

Manchester United Football Club manager, Alex Ferguson, for example, appears to have the ability to do all of these things; nurture, support, develop and, of course, turn on the famous 'Ferguson hairdrier' when he needs to stamp his authority and focus his team.

Whether you can be friends with your team will depend on the type of environment you are working in, and the type of person you are. Being friends with your colleagues and subordinates can clearly bring some benefits, but there will be some challenges along the way too.

Benefits of working with friends

- *Improved trust*. It is easier to develop a culture of trust among friends. Friends tend to do what they say they are going to do and help each other to succeed.
- *Lower levels of fear*. It is human nature to protect yourself when you are afraid. If you experience fear in the workplace, you are less likely to express your thoughts and ideas. Among friends you can be open and express ideas and concerns freely, without fear of reprisals.
- *Improved channels of communication*. Friends are far more likely to say how they see something, openly communicating and taking time to understand each other's point of view.

Difficulties of working with friends

- *Less challenging*. Friends can sometimes be less demanding of each other, focusing on what the individual may want as opposed to what the team needs.
- *Under-par performances*. Substandard performances have to be nipped in the bud and this can be especially tricky among friends.
- *Moving people on*. One of the hardest things for any manager to do is to tell an individual that they are no longer required as part of an organisation. The difficulties that such a task entails are magnified significantly between friends.

If you are the kind of person who can separate the good stuff that friendship brings from the hard stuff you might have to do as a team leader, then you will be alright. However, it might be easier to nurture a friendly environment within your team where openness and trust are valued, while at the same time maintaining some distance from colleagues, ensuring that if the hard decisions have to be made, you are able to make them.

41.   Can you beat the bully?

It would be nice to think that you could keep the playground out of the workplace. Yet, in a world which is fundamentally driven by market forces, it is no surprise that, unless constantly managed, the workplace occasionally reverts to Hobbes' nasty and brutish world, where survival of the fittest reigns, and the issue of bullying rears its ugly head.

There is a depressingly substantial volume of research that shows bullying to be rife in the workplace and, no doubt, significantly affecting the productivity and performance of companies. Take research conducted by the University of Manchester Institution of Science and Technology (UMIST), for example, which revealed that, of 5300 employees surveyed in 70 organisations, almost half reported witnessing bullying over a five-year-period. One in ten said they had been bullied in the previous six months.

There is absolutely no excuse for organisations tolerating an insidious culture of bullying. If you're being bullied at work, there are a few proactive things you can do to make the bullying stop.

Determine the grievance procedure where you work and have a word with your line manager. If the bully is your line manager, take the matter to their superior. While the thought of this may concern you, most firms will want to avoid a tribunal and will take your complaint seriously.

Don't listen to what the bully is saying. Their comments are often related to their own insecurities about themselves and their job. Keeping this in mind may help you feel better.

Avoid taking days off work because of the bully. This would partly play into their hands but, more importantly, would weaken your case when you take it to a manager. If, having complained to your firm, you still don't feel like you're getting anywhere, you could take your complaint to the Employment Tribunal Office.

Bullying is a growing problem in the UK workplace. Surprisingly, it is most widespread within the caring professions such as teaching, nursing, social services and the voluntary sector. The main problem is that those on the receiving end don't talk about it. If you are being bullied, have courage and speak up.

There are lots of people who now openly talk about being bullied when they were younger. Whitney Houston is said to have been bullied at school about her looks, as was Michelle Pfeiffer. Tom Cruise and Kevin Costner were bullied because they had to change schools a lot.

42.   Are you assertive?

CEOs and other senior executives, we tend to think, are charismatic, confident, assertive people, who have no trouble expressing their opinions or getting their point across. Not necessarily. Research into the characteristics of leader-ship by Cass Business School management academic Paul Dobson and fellow Cass academics, Noelle Irvine and Adrienne Rosen (see Question 55), has some interesting incidental findings.

Besides many qualities that are innate, such as stamina, there were a number of areas where executives could improve their prospects of reaching the top of the corporate tree. And one area where it appears that there is room for improve-ment, surprisingly, is assertiveness. Despite holding comparatively senior posi-tions in organisations, many leaders still have assertiveness issues. As Dobson points out, even people who get into senior positions may not handle difficult people and situations well, often just avoiding them, which eventually makes the situation worse.

The world famous Mayo Clinic in the US is aware of the links between poor health and a lack of assertiveness. As it points out, passive behaviour allows oth-ers to take advantage of you and signals that you do not value your own wants and needs. You may proceed on the basis that passive behaviour keeps the peace, but ultimately the price paid for keeping the peace may be a range of symptoms from high blood pressure and stress to passive aggressive behaviour.

The Mayo Clinic offers some advice via its website on how to improve your assertiveness: honestly assess your communication style; use assertive lan-guage; rehearse what you want to say; remember your body language; keep your emotions in check; and start with small wins. For more details, visit the clinic's website at www.mayoclinic.com.

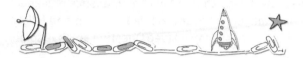

43. Are you a control freak?

'If you have a problem, if no one else can help, and if you can find them, maybe you can hire the A-Team.' Each week the narrator said these immortal words and the A-Team sprang into action on our TV screens.

Whatever situation their leader Hannibal found himself in during the 1980s action adventure series, he could only ever get out of it with the help of his team mates: Face, Murdock and B.A. Baracus. Could they complete their mission on their own? Of course not, and each did things in their own style. It was the diversity of the group that made them unique.

Sooner or later in your working life you will have to ask someone to do a task you normally would have done yourself. The great American industrialist and philanthropist Andrew Carnegie once said: 'No person will make a great business who wants to do it all himself or get all the credit.'

But when you eventually do delegate, the likelihood is that the task will be completed in a different way to how you would have done it. Will this annoy you? If so, then you perhaps haven't fully appreciated what delegation means.

Once you have accepted that you will get more done by delegating, you have to let go of a common assumption that people make. An assumption that will block the delegation process. That is, the notion that you can do it better.

Frank Flores, a leading American business executive, once said: 'Give up control even if it means the employees have to make some mistakes.'

The task will almost definitely be completed in a different way, but not necessarily in the wrong way. However, even if mistakes are made, it is your responsibility to guide and not simply take the task away. A short-term training investment will pay off in the long term, as your team develops and improves its skill set, sometimes becoming better at the task than you are yourself.

If you get it right and your team gels, you can achieve far more than you could on your own. In the words of Hannibal: 'I just love it when a plan comes together.'

44.   Is it OK to sleep on the job?

Sleeping on the job used to be a sackable offence in most companies; in many, it still is. The trouble is that the irresistible urge to take a quick nap mid-afternoon is difficult to ignore. As more of us work longer hours, the pressures of living a modern 24/7 life mean we are getting less sleep. And tired workers are costly.

An article in the January 2007 issue of the *Journal of Occupational and Environmental Medicine* says that fatigued workers cost employers $136.4 billion each year in health-related lost productive time. Lack of sleep and fatigue has been linked to corporate disasters, such as the Union Carbide chemical explosion in India, the Exxon Valdez oil spill, and the nuclear disaster at Chernobyl.

The siesta – a lunchtime or early afternoon nap – has long been a part of the national culture of some countries, particularly in hotter climates. Spain, Mexico and Italy are long standing exponents of the midday snooze. Some countries, including China, have the siesta safeguarded in law.

Medical researchers have proven that an afternoon nap can be very beneficial for the health. A six-year study in Greece found that those who took a 30-minute siesta at least three times a week had a 37 per cent lower risk of heart-related death. A NASA study revealed that a short nap can boost workers' output by as much as 34 per cent. Then there are the cognitive benefits, like increased memory.

That probably explains why some of the most brilliant minds in history have been power nappers: people like Thomas Edison, Winston Churchill, Leonardo de Vinci, Albert Einstein and John F. Kennedy.

Now, some enlightened companies are offering employees the opportunity to give in to that afternoon urge to sleep and take a power nap. Organisations are introducing napping areas, and other sleep-friendly policies.

But, until your organisation comes out in favour of dozing on company time, be careful where and when you take 40 winks. Otherwise, you may find yourself in the same plight as a Comcast employee in the US who was videoed sleeping on a customer's couch following a house call. The video was posted on YouTube, and received 227,000 hits in a short space of time. The employee was fired.

45.   Are you emotionally intelligent?

Most people have heard of IQ (intelligence quotient), the long-standing measure of intelligence, which dates back to the early 1900s and the work of French psychologist Alfred Binet. Intelligence tests measuring IQ are often employed by employers to assess job candidates.

However, for those who struggle to find the missing number in the sequence or detect the odd shape out, the good news is that, according to some researchers, there is another type of intelligence which is just as important as that measured by IQ, if not more so – emotional intelligence (EI).

Harvard scholar and psychologist, Daniel Goleman is author of the best-selling book *Emotional Intelligence* and the more recent *Social Intelligence*. 'Our emotions are hardwired into our being,' explains Goleman. 'The very architecture of the brain gives feelings priority over thought.'

In reality, it is impossible to entirely separate thought from emotion. 'We can be effective only when the two systems – our emotional brain and our thinking brain – work together,' says Goleman. 'That working relationship, which encompasses most of what we do in life, is the essence of emotional intelligence.'

Supporters of the concept point to studies suggesting that two-thirds of the abilities that set corporate star performers apart from the also-rans are based on emotional intelligence. Only one-third of the skills that matter relate to raw intelligence (as measured by IQ) and technical expertise.

How do you know if you are emotionally intelligent? Read the book. Familiarise yourself with Goleman's five domains of EI: self-awareness; managing emotions; motivating others; showing empathy; staying connected. Maybe even get a consultant to test your EQ.

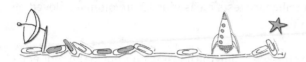

46.   Are you actively listening?

Shortly after 2pm on October 25th 1854, at the Battle of Balaclava, the Light Brigade, the elite of the British army, charged along the North Valley directly into the Russian heavy guns. Of the 673 men and officers who took part in the Charge, fewer than one hundred rode back unscathed.

Lord Raglan, who had never commanded an army in the field before, entrusted Captain Nolan with the order to charge the Russian soldiers, who were removing British guns from positions they had captured earlier in the day. The order read as follows:

'Lord Raglan wishes the cavalry to advance rapidly to the front – follow the enemy and try to prevent the enemy carrying away the guns. Troop Horse Artillery may accompany. French cavalry is on y. left. R Airey. Immediate.'

Nolan's task was to relay the order to Lord Lucan. According to Lucan, Nolan gestured towards the massed ranks of the Russian guns answering, in what Lucan described as 'a most disrespectful but significant manner', 'There, my lord, is your enemy; there are your guns.' Consequently, Lucan instructed Cardigan to lead his men towards the only guns that he could see from his position – the entrenched Russian artillery.

We have all been in situations where misunderstandings have arisen from a poor exchange of information. Most of the time, fortunately, it doesn't result in loss of life, but lost deals, broken appointments, missed meals and other mishaps.

Active listening is a listening technique that improves your understanding of the information exchange. As a result, your responses tend to be more considered, and, if both parties are able to practice active listening, a level of mutual understanding is achieved which otherwise may not be possible.

We are often in situations where we are distracted by events happening around us, or start daydreaming about tangential thoughts. Perhaps you can remember having a conversation with someone where you are focused on your intended response, rather than what the other person is saying. It happens all the time. We stop listening attentively.

Active listening means focusing absolutely on what the speaker is saying, and then, when they have finished speaking, repeating what they have said in your own words to ensure that you have understood correctly. Any discrepancies in understanding will become apparent, and the speaker can explain again.

Clearly there are times when this will just be annoying. 'Could you please pass me the salt?' 'If I understand you correctly, you feel as though you require salt on your food.'

But active listening can be very useful, helping to avoid misunderstandings and the escalation of conflict situations, for example. It will also show that you are making an effort to understand a given situation as clearly as you can, which in itself may be enough to end a conflict.

47.   Does your team need a leader?

Sick of your team leader bossing you about? How about proposing a radical new structure for your project team – no team leader. It is not as crazy as it sounds.

Professor Katherine J. Klein, of the Wharton Business School at the University of Pennsylvania, spent ten months studying medical teams in action at the Shock Trauma Centre in Baltimore. The result was a unique perspective on leadership 'as a system or a structure – a characteristic not of individuals but of the organisation or unit as a whole.'

In other words what Klein discovered was that, in the situation of the trauma unit, leadership was something that was done by different people, depending on what needed to be done at any particular time and the various skills and knowledge of the team members.

The function of the leader was separate from the many different people who fulfilled the role, depending on the circumstances. Klein also identified four key functions of the leader: providing strategic direction; monitoring team performance; instructing team members; and providing hands-on assistance when required.

Klein's research suggests that organisations would do better to set up structures to support whoever steps into a leadership position – have well established roles and clearly identified rules – than concentrate on selecting brilliant leaders.

Another example of sharing leadership responsibilities is the Australian women's hockey team – the Hockeyroos. Ric Charlesworth was appointed coach of the Hockeyroos in 1993, when the team's fortunes were at a low ebb. Charlesworth shook up the classic sports leadership model. Instead of the traditional captain, charged with motivating the team, leadership was distributed throughout the team; there was no playing captain or vice-captain.

The idea was that everyone would take responsibility for motivating team members, not just a single person. It worked. From 1994 to 2000, Charlesworth guided the Hockeyroos to two World Cups, two Olympic gold medals and a host of other trophies.

48.   Are you working with Edward Deadwood?

You know the guy. He passes off your work as his own, yet refuses to take on extra responsibility and prioritises his personal life over work.

If you do, then you won't be surprised to hear that there are lots of people with the same attitude as Mr Deadwood.

An Investors in People survey found that 75 per cent of bosses and 80 per cent of staff thought some colleagues were 'dead wood'. When they looked at the larger businesses, the statistics were even more striking. A whopping 84 per cent of workers in organisations with more than 1000 employees thought they had an underperforming colleague.

'Dead wood' employees can have an extremely detrimental impact on their colleagues, who end up working longer hours to cover for them and consequently feel undervalued. Eventually, a business runs the risk of losing their quality people, but retaining the lazy ones.

If the dead wood is someone in your team, you could talk to your colleague to explain what they are doing wrong, and the impact it has on you. If it doesn't interfere with your responsibilities, you could offer to help that person improve. You would not only be helping your colleague and your business but also yourself, as they become a more valued member of the team.

Of course, it may be that an underperforming colleague is not really dead wood at all. Perhaps they are just not clicking with the team. This type of scenario is often seen in sport. After finding success with Manchester United, Ruud van Nistelrooy had, by his own very high standards, a lean 2005/06 season. Some thought his star was fading, but the following year he moved to Real Madrid, scored 25 goals in the season, and played an important role for the team in winning the Spanish League title.

However, there will always be those who don't want to be helped and are unlikely to be motivated to look for a new challenge. They are fundamentally lazy (or worse: see Question 28) and in this case they may have to be fired. It will cost the business to do it in the short term, but in the long run cutting Mr Deadwood away may be the best thing to do.

49.   How big does your network need to be?

Big, according Marjan Bolmeijer, a CEO Coach, and CEO of Change-Leaders. com. Much bigger than you might imagine.

'You need to have a network of several hundred executives, who you know personally and who are willing to pick up the phone,' she says.

Bolmeijer, is speaking with some authority here. She has spent many years refining her approach to networking and, more recently, her use of social networking websites and online communities. A big fan of business networking website LinkedIn, Bolmeijer has the seventh largest network on the website. Her first level connections number over 17,500 and rising; her second level connections total 1.3 million plus.

And that's comparatively small fry compared to Ron Bates, managing principal of Executive Advance Group, who is probably the most networked man on the planet. Bates boasts 32,340 connections on LinkedIn (many more by the time this goes to print, no doubt). It is not known if he phones them all on a regular basis.

These kinds of numbers may be out of reach for many, and of practical use to only a few, but Bolmeijer's point about numbers makes sense. 'It might seem like a high number, but at certain times, when you need your network the most, when you are in transition and looking for a new position, for example, that network can turn out to be really small,' she says.

Bolmeijer also has some tips for social network users. Never change your phone number, or your email address, she says. Make sure your email address goes next to your name, and put as much information about yourself in your profile as possible. She also cautions against messing up. As she points out – bad news travels fast through your network.

50.   Are you having a laugh?

There is a long tradition of laughing at the nature of work and the absurdities of working life. In 1955 in *Parkinson's Law: The Pursuit of Progress*, C. Northcote Parkinson stated Parkinson's Law: 'Work expands so as to fill the time available for its completion.' In a later book, *The Law and the Profits*, he introduced Parkinson's Second Law: 'Expenditure rises to meet income.'

Canadian author Laurence Peter wrote *The Peter Principle*, published in 1969. In it Peter offers his take on career progression, namely that managers in an organisation rise to their level of incompetence, by being promoted until they fail to do well. 'For each individual, for you, for me, the final promotion is from a level of competence to a level of incompetence,' wrote Peter. He also offered an acerbic take on consultants: 'They are the people who borrow your watch to tell you what time it is and then walk off with it.'

Today's antidotes to the banality of corporate speak and management pomposity are of course Dilbert, the creation of US cartoonist Scott Adams, and David Brent, the fictional star of Ricky Gervais' play-it-straight sitcom, *The Office*.

In the workplace itself, however, humour has had an uneasy ride. In the 1930s and 1940s, at Ford Motor Company in the US, laughing was considered a disciplinary offence. Humming and whistling were frowned upon. At the famous River Rouge, one employee, John Gallo, was fired because he was 'caught in the act of smiling', having earlier been caught 'laughing with the other fellows'. Dangerous stuff.

Today, corporate attitudes towards humour in the workplace appear to have changed. In 2005, ice-cream makers Ben & Jerry's announced the appointment of Walt Freese, to the position of Chief Euphoria Officer. Southwest Airlines in the US has built decades of outstanding success on creating a culture of fun.

Organisations shouldn't take the task of injecting some humour into the workplace too light-heartedly. Research by David Abramis, an organisational psychologist and Professor of Management at California State University, Long Beach, has shown that people who have fun at work are more productive.

51.   Can you smooch in the storeroom?

A chance encounter by the coffee machine, canoodling in the cubicle, a few furtive emails, and before you know it you are in a relationship with a work colleague. Everyone knows that it isn't the smartest thing to do, but it is hardly surprising that, when people spend so much time at work, Cupid's bow occasionally finds its mark.

Research by RPCushing Recruitment found that 20 per cent of office workers have had an office fling, 15 per cent admitted to having a crush on someone in their office and a whopping two thirds said they have had a sexual fantasy about a colleague in the past.

The three aspects of a work relationship that will really bother your boss are the potential for abuse, the potential for alliance, and the potential for distraction. It is with these issues in mind that more and more UK companies are starting to follow their US counterparts by setting up 'anti-dating' clauses in employment terms.

They are also concerned about sexual harassment claims if the marriage or relationship breaks down. These types of clauses are very difficult to enforce, but if you want to keep your job, what do you do when you are bitten by the love bug?

- *No canoodling on company time.* This means the virtual stuff as well as in reality. No risqué emails and definitely no smooching in the storeroom.
- *Avoid joint business trips.* And definitely don't book a double room. It can be seen as spending the company's money to progress your relationship.

- *Don't get tied up.* (Not like that.) If your behaviour explicitly goes against company policy, don't get entangled in an argument with them. Be discreet, be professional and keep your job.

We will leave you with this final thought. If you need to have another excuse to keep your desk cluttered and overflowing with paperwork, the same RPCushing survey found that one in ten UK workers claim they have had sex in the office. Don't let your desk be an option.

Section 4: Climbing the ladder

- Can you have a better car than your boss?
- Anyone for golf?
- Are you a workplace warrior?
- Do you have to be 'nasty' to get to the top?
- Leader or manager?
- Why would you turn down a promotion?
- MBA or no MBA?
- Is the glass ceiling unbreakable?
- Which business books should you read (apart from this one, of course)?
- Who is your role model?
- Will your job be outsourced?
- How do you say goodbye?
- Do you have what it takes?
- How many Vice Presidents do you need to make a company?

52.   Can you have a better car than your boss?

Is your boss more concerned with bling and baubles than whether you have the appropriate training? Do they spend most of their time looking at themselves in the mirror when they are dictating a memo? If so, it is likely that they won't like you showing them up when you both head out of the building any more than if you did it in the office itself.

With offers from car leasing companies available to individuals as well as the traditional deals to businesses, you could trade in your battered old run-around for something with a little more class and leave your boss in a cloud of dust as you exit the car park. But will you still have your job by the time it comes to make the second payment on your new wheels?

In theory, parking your Ferrari next to the middle-of-the-range BMW your boss drives shouldn't lose you your job. Or turning up with a Hermes Birkin handbag. Or flashing your gold Bentley Mulliner Tourbillon wristwatch. In theory. It may spark a degree of envy, however, which, if accompanied by any of the following, may leave your boss pondering why they employed you in the first place.

- *Being late*. Few things will annoy your boss more than keeping them waiting, giving the impression that your time is more valuable than theirs.
- *Reneging on commitments*. Leaving assignments only partially completed will add to your boss' workload.
- *Taking too many breaks*. Repeated breaks for cigarettes, coffee, toilet, etc. will make it seem that you spend more time away from your desk than at it.
- *Not taking responsibility*. Always passing the buck and blaming your boss?

- *Disagreeing with your boss in public.* No one likes being made to look stupid.

Having scanned this list of misdemeanours, you are probably thinking you are safe and that the simple act of having a better car than your boss won't cause you any trouble. Well don't be so sure. In Vista, San Diego County, a woman sued her former employer after her manager fired her on the spot when she saw the woman's car had a bumper sticker advertising '1360 Air America Progressive Talk Radio'. The reason her boss gave: 'The country is on a high state of alert. For all I know, you could be al-Qaida.'

Be warned: some bosses are touchy.

In case you are wondering about overstepping the mark, *What Car 2007* produced the following executive car league table.

1	Lexus IS
2=	BMW 3 Series
2=	Jaguar S-type
4	Volvo V70
5=	Mercedes C-Class
5=	Mercedes E-Class
5=	MG Rover 75/ZT
8	Jaguar X-type
9	Audi A6
10	Audi A4

53.   Anyone for golf?

The sport most popularly associated with executives is, of course, golf. Companies have been bought and sold, fortunes made and won, careers built and broken on the fairways and greens of the world's golf courses.

Golf and big business seem inseparable. Here are just a few business titans who have had some connection with a golf course.

Financial services pioneer Charles Schwab caddied as boy, after selling walnuts, eggs, and chickens – he was an enterprising child. Warren Buffett, the billionaire investor, collected lost golf balls and sold them. John H. Patterson, founder of National Cash Registers, had a golf course on his private estate, which employees were allowed to use. Milton Hershey, the chocolate bar tycoon, built an entire town for his employees, complete with golf course – it was to be called Hersheyoko, following a naming competition, but the US postal service didn't approve, so he went for Hershey Town instead.

Scott McNealy, founder of Sun Microsystems, is an excellent golfer. McNealy captained his university golf team and, when CEO, was ranked No.1 in *Golf Digest* magazine's bi-annual Fortune 500 company CEO golf rankings (now *Fortune 1000* CEOs), for three consecutive rankings. The current No.1 is James R. Crane of Eagle Global Logistics. The legendary tycoon Howard Hughes may not have played golf, but he did try to land an XF-11 experimental reconnaissance aircraft on the Los Angeles Country Club golf course. Fortunately for the green keeper, but not Hughes, he didn't quite make it, ploughing through a couple of houses instead.

As well as ranking the CEOs, *Golf Digest* also surveys them. Among other things, the 2006 survey revealed that: 38 per cent admit to having bent the rules; 93 per cent play more than 20 rounds a year and 57 per cent more than 30; 71 per cent have ended up doing business with someone met on a round of golf; 100 per cent say that they have never seen a subordinate let them win; encouragingly, not one said that they would prefer to play at the Augusta National than post a record profit.

Not all employees have it so easy when it comes to networking with the boss, though. Spare a thought for the senior executives at Siebel, when founder Tom Siebel was at the helm. One of Siebel's favourite pastimes? Roping cattle.

54.   Are you a workplace warrior?

Everyone knows business is war, right? Hence all the tough talk, amidst the competitive hurly burly, about destroying the opposition.

In the past, some companies have taken the war metaphor a little too literally. The Hanseatic League, an alliance of cities in northern Germany, for example, originally set up as a trading organisation in the 15th century, but ended up in naval wars with various nations. Equally, the East India Company, formed to take advantage of British trading concessions in India, under the command of Sir Robert Clive, fought the local Indian rulers as well as the French.

Today, modern executives like to mix their military philosophy and business by applying the strategies of Sun-Tzu's *The Art of War*, written 2500 years ago. Confusion surrounds the origins of the book. Some attribute it to Sun Wu, a military general alive around 500 BC. The book's title is *Sun Tzu Ping Fa*, which can be literally translated as 'The military method of venerable Mr Sun'.

What is certain is that executives the world over have lapped up advice, such as: 'Deploy forces to defend the strategic points; exercise vigilance in preparation, do not be indolent. Deeply investigate the true situation, secretly await their laxity. Wait until they leave their strongholds, then seize what they love.' Or: 'To subdue the enemy's forces without fighting is the summit of skill. The best approach is to attack the other side's strategy; next best is to attack his alliances; next best is to attack his soldiers; the worst is to attack cities.'

That model of corporate capitalism, Gordon Gekko, was a fan. 'I don't throw darts at a board. I bet on sure things,' he says in the movie *Wall Street*. 'Read Sun-Tzu, *The Art of War*. Every battle is won before it is ever fought.'

Another avid follower is fictional Mafia boss Tony Soprano:

'Been reading that – that book you told me about. You know, *The Art of War* by Sun Tzu. I mean, here's this guy, a Chinese general, wrote this thing 2400 years ago, and most of it still applies today! ... You know most of the guys that I know, they read Prince Machiavelli, and I had Carmela go and get *The Cliff Notes* once and – he's okay. But this book is much better about strategy.'

So if you see your colleague with a well-thumbed copy of *The Art of War*, take care – especially when leaving your stronghold.

55.   Do you have to be 'nasty' to get to the top?

We all know what it takes to get to the top of the corporate career ladder and stay there – or at least we think we do. For starters: hard work, luck, a copy of Machiavelli's *The Prince*, and the equivalent of a Masters degree in office politics. Isn't it always the office backstabbers and plotters who clamber up the greasy promotion pole, then ruthlessly maintain their grip on the top spot?

Not according to recent research by Paul Dobson, senior lecturer in organisational behaviour at Cass Business School, and fellow Cass academics Noelle Irvine and Adrienne Rosen. The good news for those who like to believe in corporate karma and don't know their Machiavelli from their Metallica is that being nice (plus possessing a few other characteristics like fierce ambition and outstanding stamina) is a winning career strategy.

The research, in which 35 senior CEOs from 17 different industries were interviewed about 210 of their peers, led to a list of the key determinants of sustained success, plus a questionnaire: *The Chief Executive Success Predictor*.

One of the most important distinguishing characteristics of the really successful corporate leaders is their interpersonal skills. 'They are described as being fun and interesting to be with, they are charismatic,' says Dobson. 'Their mastery of interpersonal skills enables them to build and maintain networks over time with key business shareholders, such as banks, government departments, clients and competitors.'

Perhaps the most interesting insight, though, concerns how the best leaders relate to other people. 'Some people think you have to fight tooth and nail to get to the top, backstabbing as you go, but that is not what the research tells us,' says Dobson. 'The successful leaders who get to the top and stay there are not the Machiavellian archetypes. People often behave in certain ways because they have the wrong idea about how to get on in an organisation. This research might help correct misperceptions, particularly about trust and working with people, about playing straight as opposed to playing politics. It might help change people's mental models about what leads to success.'

56.   Leader or manager?

Why would anyone want to be a drab, boring manager? 'Manager' has become something of a dirty word in recent years, associated with the performance of dull administrative tasks, and not very career-friendly. Much better to be a dashing, heroic, go-getting, exciting leader, driving transformation and change from the top (even if it isn't really needed).

The word management originates from the French *ménagement* – the art of conducting or directing. Mary Parker Follett, a leading management theorist in the 1920s, defined management as 'the art of getting things done through people'. It has also been defined as: 'the attainment of organisational goals in an effective and efficient manner through planning, organising, leading and controlling organisational resources.'

The study of management is relatively new. Business schools are a little over a century old. Management theory got underway in earnest in the late 19th century and early 20th centuries, with the work of individuals such as Henri Fayol, Frederick W. Taylor and Alfred Sloan.

Leadership theory, however, has a much longer history. The study of leadership dates back to the ancient world, when the lives of the Roman emperors were analysed to identify common traits which marked individuals as destined for leadership. It is only in the 19th and 20th centuries that the leadership spotlight has turned on the CEO – rather than kings, generals, politicians and religious leaders.

Yet, while the idea of the charismatic corporate CEO as a leader has been feted over the last few decades, there are signs that management and the role of the manager is becoming more fashionable.

Organisations are stripping out hierarchies, becoming flatter and more networked. In these types of organisation, people will need the ability to persuade, influence and convince, rather than tell and order. Step forward the manager; your organisation needs you.

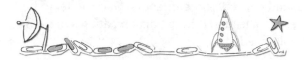

57.   Why would you turn down a promotion?

You work hard, you are an asset to your company and your bosses appreciate your effort. Sooner or later, you are likely to be offered a promotion and surely you jump at the opportunity. Or do you?

A survey conducted by NBC produced some rather surprising statistics. Out of almost 3500 participants, 79 per cent of those asked said that they would turn down a promotion if it were offered to them. Here are the top five reasons:

- 27 per cent said they don't want any more responsibility
- 23 per cent cited family obligations as their reason
- 17 per cent said that they hated managing people
- 9.7 per cent said they loved their current job and wouldn't want to change
- 2.8 per cent had concerns about failing that would stop them moving up the ladder

In the past, it was unthinkable that someone would refuse a promotion even if it meant relocating their family. It would have signalled the end of your career.

However, as the statistics show, this is no longer the case. As more people focus on their work-life balance, employers are starting to realise that it is OK for employees to make that choice.

But do you run the risk of losing some respect from career-focused peers within the business? The key to turning down a promotion is to communicate that decision well. Here is a three-step solution to turning them down while, at the same time, maintaining respect.

1   Thank your boss for considering you worthy of promotion and tell them why you believe a promotion is not right for you or the company.
2   Tell them that, by you staying in your current position, you will continue to be able to make the best contribution to the company's success.
3   Offer to assist in other areas that further highlight that they were right to consider you for a promotion, but which won't compromise the reasons why you didn't take it.

58.   MBA or no MBA?

Opinions on whether an MBA is necessary or desirable at the upper echelons of management are sharply divided. However, there is little doubt that having an MBA provides a salary lift – more so if the MBA is taken at a top-ranked school.

According to the Association of MBAs in the UK (AMBA), an MBA from a leading business school is highly valued by recruiters and has a huge impact on earnings potential. AMBA's Career Survey 2006 states that MBA graduates can expect an average base salary increase of 20 per cent after graduation, with base salary continuing to increase sharply, particularly between three and five years after graduation. The average salary post MBA is £65,000 plus variable remuneration.

Increasingly the MBA is seen as a point of differentiation, especially as candidates with first degrees are more commonplace today than twenty years ago. In April 2001, *Fortune* magazine published the advanced degrees of the leading CEOs of the Fortune 200: MBAs (79); joint degrees and LLBs (15); PhDs (12); MDs (2); and other graduate degree (18).

There are many corporate big-hitters who possess an MBA. About 30 per cent of CEOs running the USA's largest 1000 companies have an MBA. Notable MBAs from the corporate world include: John Chambers (Cisco); Fred Smith (founder, Federal Express); Steve Ballmer (CEO, Microsoft); Arthur Rock (Venture Capital pioneer); Meg Whitman (CEO, eBay); and Phil Knight (co-founder, Nike).

Of course there are many more that don't.

59.   Is the glass ceiling unbreakable?

On 1 January 2006, a new law came into effect in Norway: women must hold at least 40 per cent of the seats on the boards of publicly listed Norwegian companies. The intention is to accelerate the elevation of women into the boardroom and the c-suite (CEOs, CFOs, COOs, etc.). While the move has attracted criticism, judging by recent figures, action is required. Organisations may claim that they are championing diversity, but when it comes to promoting women to the top jobs, the statistics tell a different story.

A 2007 report, *Women Board Directors in the Fortune Global 200 Companies*, published by Corporate Women Directors International (CWDI), revealed that women held just 11.2 per cent of posts at the top of the 200 largest companies in the world. And, in those companies with female board representation, 45.6 per cent had just one woman on the board.

Europe lags behind the US in what little moves there are to appoint women directors. The list of the top companies with the highest percentage of women board directors featured 18 US-based companies, with eight from Europe. The top two spots were taken by Netherlands-headquartered firm Royal Ahold, where women held four out of the seven seats on the supervisory board, and Norway's Statoil, with five out of ten board members being women.

In Asia, the picture is worse for women with career aspirations to break the glass ceiling. Only five out of 389 board seats at Fortune Global 200 companies in Japan were held by women. Of the 45 companies without any female representation, 30 were Asian companies, including major brands such as Toyota, Nissan Motor, Hyundai, and Honda, as well as some major European corporations such as DaimlerChrysler, and Fiat.

For those women who do make it to the top, the news is not good either. UK academics Alexander Haslam and Michelle Ryan analysed a correlation of the performance of FTSE 100 companies in the UK during 2003, with and without women on their boards. Their conclusion was that companies performing badly are more likely to appoint women to the board. Once performance recovers, companies are less likely to appoint women to the board. As a result, women directors are often appointed at a difficult period and their appointment can easily be mistaken for a factor in the company's poor performance.

In other words, suggested Haslam and Ryan, even when women do break through the unbreakable glass ceiling they typically confront when climbing the corporate ladder, they often find themselves at the edge of a glass cliff.

Back in Norway, positive action is having a big effect on board diversity. Of the 520 public limited companies caught by the legislation, 55 per cent now meet the 40 per cent requirement.

60. Which business books should you read (apart from this one, of course)?

There are several ways you can approach this question. A good place to start is Stuart Crainer's *The Ultimate Business Library: The Greatest Books That Made Management*. After all, why read the greatest books in management literature when you can read an excellent summary of them all, and in one book?

Today the market for business books is huge – just check out the business shelves in your local bookstore. But it wasn't always this way. Interest in management writing on today's scale is a comparatively recent phenomenon.

As Crainer notes, the book that made management books popular is *In Search of Excellence* by Thomas J. Peters and Robert H. Waterman, two McKinsey and Company consultants. Its publication in October 1982 was a milestone in business publishing. The authors sold 25,000 copies direct to the public in its first year, before the book was picked up by a mainstream publisher. It has since sold over six million.

Crainer's book on books contains the seminal works of the management oeuvre, from that early pot-boiler by proto-computer inventor Charles Babbage, *On the Economy of Machinery & Manufactures* (1832), past the managerial fascism of Frederick W. Taylor's *The Principles of Scientific Management* (1911), and on to the modern-day classic *Built to Last* (1994) by James Collins and Jerry Porras.

An alternative approach to compiling a business book reading list might be to take a ranking of management gurus, such as the Thinkers 50, produced by Suntop Media, or a similar list of gurus from consultancy firm Accenture, and then work your way through books produced by the gurus listed.

Or you could just start with possibly one of the most popular management books ever written – *The Dilbert Principle* by Scott Adams. (The Dilbert Principle states that the most ineffective workers will be moved to a place where they can do the least damage – management.)

61.   Who is your role model?

Ask people who their role model is and you will get a variety of answers. Children's BBC conducted a poll where Bart Simpson came out top; YouGov's poll determined that Richard Branson was the number one business role model; others choose Bruce Lee, Tiger Woods, Jane Fonda … the list goes on and on. Some may choose Eminem who, in the lyrics of 'Role Model', set out virtually everything that a role model shouldn't be.

But focusing on an 'anti role model' could get a little confusing, so let's determine what a role model actually is. Role models have qualities that we admire, can learn from and would like to have. We don't arrive in the world with an innate knowledge of how best to live our lives. We need guidance from somewhere. A good role model will help you stay motivated as you strive to achieve greater things.

There are numerous places where you can find role models. Children often see their parents as role models and are influenced throughout their life by the examples picked up from them. Celebrities are the first choice for some people as they can provide a focus and help you determine your goals, but beware: they are just as likely to infuriate as to inspire.

Role models can be colleagues with whom you have worked, an acquaintance you met in a bar or a long-standing friend. Take the best each of them has to offer and they will provide you with a rich source of insight and guidance.

To help you find your role models, answer these questions:

- *In what area of your life would you benefit from a role model?* The clearer you are about what area of your life you would like guidance with, the easier it will be to find the right role model for you.
- *Is there someone from within your circle of friends who would be a good role model?* Consider your network of friends and determine who is best placed to help you.
- *Is the person you have chosen actually the best person for you?* Regularly check that your role model is the best person for you to model yourself on; you may outgrow them.

Kevin Johnson, the former NBA Basketball star, had this to say: 'My role model was my grandfather. He instilled in me the feeling that, no matter how successful you are, you have a responsibility to help others.'

62.   Will your job be outsourced?

In September 2006, fashion company Burberry announced there would be a period of consultation following its proposal to close its clothing factory in Treorchy, Wales. Continuing operations at the plant was not commercially viable,

Burberry said. The plant was closed despite protests, and the jobs moved to China.

The Burberry case is an indication of the impact that outsourcing (and off-shoring, where the work is moved to another country) can have on people's lives. The reality is, if your job is capable of being outsourced, it probably will be – eventually. As many people have discovered to their cost, we live, and work, in a global economy. Organisations can source different parts of their value chain – the chain of processes that link the raw goods with the sale of the finished materials – from anywhere in the world. Why pay UK wage rates to deliver a customer service from a call centre in Slough, if you can pay much lower salaries to people manning a call centre in India, and still maintain the same or a better standard of performance?

Outsourcing is nothing new. It started with manufacturing, progressed through IT services, business processes, and human resources, and now encompasses a wide range of corporate functions. It is a huge multi-billion dollar market. Contrary to public perception, however, some western economies, such as the UK, sell more outsourcing services than they buy.

Ultimately, differentials in labour costs may even go up, removing a major incentive for outsourcing. Until then, the volume of jobs outsourced offshore and the scope of activities are likely to expand. The destination of the outsourced activities is also likely to shift, as companies constantly search for the optimal service provision, taking into account factors like quality of service and cost.

Some people are relatively safe from the risk of seeing their job outsourced. It is, theoretically at least, possible to do a limited medical consultation remotely using modern teleconferencing technologies, just as it is possible to diagnose X-ray images from the UK in Bangalore, India, or Shanghai, China. It is not, how-ever, possible to cut hair or build a house without being physically present. Jobs that require physical proximity to the consumer are safe from outsourcing, for the time being.

63.   How do you say goodbye?

Buster Martin got his first job in 1916, at the age of ten, running errands in the Brixton market; he then did numerous other jobs, including stints in both the army and the navy. In 2007, at the ripe old age of 100, he was still working, cleaning vans for a plumbing firm in London.

If you are lucky enough to be able to work until you are 100, the chances are you will have had a variety of jobs. Few people enter the job market nowadays expecting to be with the same organisation for 30 years.

In 2000, the American Bureau of Labour Statistics found that the average number of jobs someone was likely to have in a twenty-year period was over nine, and this looks likely to increase. So the chances are that you are going to have to part company with your current employer at some point – but what is the right way to do it?

With the job market being so fluid and with so many people jumping from one organisation to another, it is vital that you exit a job in the right manner. Not only does a smooth departure help your current colleagues cope but, as you are likely to cross paths with them at some point in the future, your reputation will not be tainted.

Here's what the experts suggest:

*   *Notice*. Your company will expect a certain amount of notice that you are leaving: make sure that you give them this much as a minimum. This will normally be between 2 and 4 weeks.

- *Commit*. Stay focused on your duties and commitments and make sure that any outstanding issues are dealt with before your departure.
- *Train*. Offer to help train your replacement, assisting your employer to make the transition.
- *Benefit*. Know what you are entitled to in terms of benefits owed to you, unused holiday, pension, etc.
- *Be discreet*. Whatever your reasons for leaving, keep them to yourself.
- *Contact*. Stay in touch with the movers and shakers within the business.
- *Thank*. Say thank you to your co-workers and your boss.

Of course, you may decide that staying with the same company for 30 years is indeed right for you, but if you are planning on emulating Buster, you would have to do that three times before you caught up with his impressive working record.

64.   Do you have what it takes?

Despite the possible rise of the manager, leadership skills are still in huge demand in organisations. The cult of the CEO lives on. Business schools emphasise the efforts they make to develop leadership skills to potential MBA participants. Thousands of books are published on how to become a great/effective/quiet/visionary leader.

For all those with half a mind on career progression, it is worth keeping up with the latest leadership theories, if only so that you can namecheck a few leadership gurus, and mention a few key terms, when talking to your boss.

Recent leadership theories include 'the crucible of leadership' from Warren Bennis; 'Level 5 leadership' from Jim Collins; Rob Goffee and Gareth Jones on authentic leadership; and 'tipping point leadership' from W. Chan Kim and Renee Mauborgne.

Each has persuasive elements. Level 5 leadership is a potent blend of self-lessness, humility and iron will, exhibited by typically 'quiet leaders' rather than the larger-than-life figures associated with organisational transformation. Au-thentic leadership holds that the best leaders make the most of the qualities they already possess. They trade on their strengths and understand their weaknesses. To be useful, these qualities must be real, perceived by others and significant.

'Crucibles' are 'utterly transforming events or tests that individuals must pass through and make meaning from in order to learn, grow, and lead.' Thus leaders are shaped by significant events such as corporate crises. Tipping point leader-ship is built around four elements: the cognitive (communicating and ensuring managers are in touch with the problems); politics (keeping internal foes quiet and isolating external ones); resources (initially concentrating on trouble areas); and motivation (matching messages to various levels within the organisation).

Other leadership terms and people worth mentioning (and studying, time permitting): Great Man and trait theory; transformational and transactional leader-ship; Meredith Belbin and team leadership; Jim Kouzes and Barry Posner and the leader as a catalyst for change; Peter Senge and the leader as a strategic visionary; Rakesh Khurana and the irrational quest for charismatic CEOs; Michael Maccoby and narcissistic leadership and the bonds between follower and leader.

Regarding putting it into action; it will be difficult. Given that there are a number of divergent views, it would be impossible to put them all into action simultaneously. Of course, you might try one theory one week, and a different one the next. But then that is hardly authentic, is it?

65.   How many Vice Presidents do you need to make a company?

Quite a lot, it seems. In America at least, where a cursory glance down the executive ranks of most companies reveals a Vice President or VP (veep) at every turn.

Why the plethora of veeps (is that the collective noun)? Several reasons. In small companies, a layer of VPs makes the CEO feel more important. It also, in any size company, makes the VP feel more important. It looks good on the business card, after all. Plus, with flatter hierarchies, how do you differentiate people? Simple: give them a title – as opposed to a wage rise.

Even the much-vaunted c-suite (CEO, CFO, COO, etc.) has been hit by what Wharton Business School management academics have termed 'title inflation'.

There used to be a time when there was the Chief Executive Officer, the Chief Financial Officer and, well, that was often it. Today, it seems that there are almost as many chiefs as employees. Yahoo has Chief Yahoos – the two founders – Chief People Yahoo, a Chief Strategy Officer, a Chief Accounting Officer, and assorted other chiefs.

That's only scraping the surface of chiefdom. Chiefs also count among their ranks the following titles: Chief Blogging Officer, Chief Experience Officer, Chief Innovation Officer, Chief Visionary Officer ... even Chief Happiness Officer.

Where will it stop? For the foreseeable future, as organisations become flatter and hierarchies are stripped out, it is likely that people will seek identity through increasingly niche titles.

Chief Vice President anyone?

Section 5: Rags to riches

- What is the most lavish corporate perk?
- Gone phishing?
- What is the best-paid job in the world?
- How easy is it to become a billionaire?
- Which country has the highest taxes?
- Should you keep it in the family?
- Can you fiddle your expenses?
- Is anything as safe as houses?
- How do you ask for a bank loan?
- What happens when investors go mad?
- Hacked off?
- Is everyone to blame?
- What is the worst-paid job in the world?

66. What is the most lavish corporate perk?

What's the point of being successful if you can't have a few perks? Whether it's a plane, a case of vintage wine, or a few days out in the corporate box at a football game, it is always nice to know you are appreciated.

How about a private airplane, for example? When it comes to air travel, the sleek jets made by Gulfstream and Lear are the most popular with CEOs – but in the world of outrageous wealth, there is always someone with something bigger and better. Unless of course, you are Roman Abramovich, one of Russia's most powerful businessmen and owner of Chelsea Football Club. Abramovich has a Boeing 767–300, equipped with the usual add-ons, plus a few extras such as a missile jammer. A basic Boeing 767 has a price tag of $100 million – not cheap – and then there is the missile jammer, which costs in the region of $1.5 million. The 767 goes nicely – matching paint livery – with the Boeing Business Jet 737 Abramovich also owns.

Sometimes the perks senior executives receive are made by the company they work for, and are not always what you would want, or need. For example, the executives at Goodyear Tire & Rubber Co. can get up to two sets of tyres a year. Reynolds American Inc. executives get free cigarettes and chewing tobacco. At Anheuser-Busch, the execs get free beer.

There are occasions when workers further down the hierarchy also get to sample the pleasure of a lavish corporate perk. At a cost of $3.2 million, UK tycoon Sir Richard Branson bought Makepeace Island off Australia's Queensland Sunshine Coast as a leisure haven for staff of his Virgin companies worldwide.

Corporate perks are not a new phenomenon. In April 1913, Woolworths Corporate offices were moved into the Woolworth Building, the tallest building in the world at the time. Frank Woolworth, who commissioned the building costing $13.5 million, paid in cash and settled into his office situated on the 24th floor. Thirty feet square, its design was based on Napoleon's famous Empire Room and contained the clock and other articles from the original room. Try getting that through on expenses.

67.   Gone phishing?

No matter who you are, and what you want to keep private, it seems that there is always someone who is trying to get into your system, steal your passwords and retire to the Bahamas on the profits.

Even if you are sitting smugly in an air-conditioned office somewhere, don't assume that your information is safe. A survey conducted by Cyber-Ark Software discovered that a third of all IT workers abuse their access to company systems by looking at confidential information, including private files, wage data, and the personal emails of their colleagues.

There are other ways to lose out in this age of information transfer. Rarely a day goes by when the email inbox isn't inundated with pleas from an unfortunate prince, of a country you can't remember your geography teacher ever mentioning, asking for your assistance in handling his millions of pounds.

Follow the instructions and you will end up handing over your bank details to some cyber criminal holed up in another country (one you probably have heard of this time).

This crafty internet practice of duping you into handing over your personal information is called phishing. And despite the fact that most people reading this are aware that it happens, some people are still being ripped off.

It's not just individuals getting caught out; companies are being targeted too. Recent research by insurers Royal & Sun Alliance (R&SA) and the Centre for Economics and Business Research (CEBR) reveals that the cost to UK firms of corporate identity (ID) theft is due to hit £700 million a year by 2020. And, just like personal identity theft, the corporate kind gives the cyber crooks the ability to withdraw money from bank accounts and exploit lines of credit.

Scams like contacting Companies House to change company details so that they can act in the name of a company mean that companies need to be ever more vigilant when it comes to security: running security checks on new employees; shredding documents; securing digital passwords; buying up the various permutations of internet domain names to prevent misuse by phishers; and signing up to a Companies House service that notifies companies if a request to change company details is made.

Unfortunately, even before you have set up your firewalls, email filters and security procedures, the phishers are moving on to their next campaign against the unsuspecting: smishing. That's phishing on your cell phone. So the next time a text message arrives telling you that you are signed up to an online store, and that if you don't visit the website listed it will cost you £10 per week, ignore it.

68.   What is the best-paid job in the world?

More money might not make you happier or healthier but, if your goal is to make a lot of money, you probably need to make your career choice fairly early on in life.

Top lawyers and medics earn good salaries. A QC might earn in excess of £1 million, as can partners of leading solicitors. In healthcare, some general practitioners might earn in excess of £250,000.

For the big money you should head for the City and the world of finance. Hedge funds are where the serious money is at the moment. In 2006, the three top hedge-fund earners each took home over $1 billion. The top 25 averaged $570 million.

The huge salaries for the top hedge-fund managers make earnings for sports stars and Hollywood film actors pale into insignificance. In the UK's Premier Football League, top earners might bring in £130,000 a week – not to be dismissed, but still some way behind the City's biggest earners. In the US, the highest paid NFL players earn around $20 million, although there is a salary cap in most US sports.

In Hollywood, top stars like Tom Cruise, Will Ferrell and Tom Hanks can earn around $20m but, if they can negotiate a points deal, taking some of the profits, they may earn much more. Marlon Brando was paid almost $3.4 million, plus points, for the 1978 film *Superman* and its sequel. He never appeared in the sequel, due to a dispute, and eventually earned $14 million for 12 shooting days and about 10 minutes screen-time.

There are other ways to strike it rich, although a regular salary might be out of the question. George Carmack and Skookum Jim struck gold in the Yukon Valley Alaska in 1896, sparking the Klondike goldrush. By the time the hundreds of thousands of prospectors had arrived, Carmack had already extracted over a ton of gold.

A discovery of a scarce natural resource, such as the gold in the Yukon, doesn't always yield such lucrative results, though. In 1893, an African worker at the Jagersfontein in South Africa was shovelling gravel onto a truck when he discovered a huge rough diamond. He hid the diamond, giving it directly to the mine manager. The Excelsior diamond, at 995.2 metric carats, was one of the largest rough diamonds ever to have been discovered. The gem was eventually cut into 21 smaller stones, the largest of which reappeared on the market in 1996, when it was bought for $2,642,000. The worker was rewarded with £500 plus a horse, complete with saddle and bridle.

69.   How easy is it to become a billionaire?

Not that easy. But easier than it used to be. There are more billionaires than ever, from more nations than ever. The annual look at billionaires in *Forbes* magazine revealed 946 billionaires in 2007, with 178 newly minted billionaires joining the list.

While the average age of billionaires is coming down, it still takes time to accumulate such riches – 62 years on average. Two-thirds of all that wealth is self-made from scratch. And the rich are getting richer, with total net wealth up by $900 billion to $3.5 trillion. That's more than the UK's annual GDP.

By the time this book is published the richest man on the planet is likely to be either Microsoft founder Bill Gates, or Mexican telecoms magnate Carlos Slim Helú, with investment guru Warren Buffett close behind.

The UK's not the best place to become a millionaire though; the majority of the world's billionaires come from the US, with close to 30 in the UK. In terms of newcomers, the best place to be is Russia.

As for how billionaires make their money, the *Forbes* list covers just about every business sector. You could write a bestseller, like J. K. Rowling did, corner the world's computing operating systems, like Bill Gates, or venture into flat pack furniture, as per IKEA's Ingvar Kamprad.

Interestingly, both Kamprad and Buffett, two of the four richest people on the planet, are famously frugal. Buffett, for example, still lives in the house he bought in 1958 for $31,500. The thrifty Kamprad, who once described himself as a 'Swedish Scotsman', flies economy, eats modestly, dresses casually and has been known to haggle at his local market.

70.   Which country has the highest taxes?

As Benjamin Franklin said: 'In this world, nothing is certain but death and taxes.' So if you have made it into the ranks of the globally mobile, where the retention of your hard-earned cash is a bigger priority than the view from your living room window, you will want to work out who is going to nibble the biggest chunk out of your income in the form of taxes.

For example, a Danish or Swedish executive can expect to lose almost 60 per cent of their income in tax, whereas in Qatar, there is no income tax deduction.

The 2007 *Forbes* Tax Misery Index has the following countries at the top of the list when it comes to taking a big bite out of your pay check:

- France
- China
- Belgium
- Sweden
- Italy
- Austria
- Poland
- Spain
- Argentina
- Slovenia

And at the top of the *Forbes* Happiness index the countries which let you keep the largest majority of your income:

- United Arab Emirates
- Hong Kong
- Cyprus
- Georgia
- Singapore
- Russia
- Taiwan
- Thailand
- South Africa
- The Philippines

71.   Should you keep it in the family?

Despite the inevitable fears of errant offspring destroying all the hard work of the business founder, family businesses have a remarkably impressive performance record.

Some of the most famous corporations in the world are, or have been, long-standing family firms. In the US, familiar family firms include Marriott, Mars, Levi Strauss, Weyerhaeuser, Wal-Mart and Wrigley. In Europe, family firms include J. Sainsbury, Aldi, Fiat, Michelin and Ikea. Family firms are particularly popular in Asia, including companies like LG Group, Samsung, Matsushita, Toyota and the Tata Group, to name a few.

A study published in *Business Week* in 2003 looked at family firms in the Standard & Poor's 500, where the founders or their families maintained a presence in management, on the board or as significant shareholders. Over the previous decade, family businesses outperformed non-family businesses, with an average return to shareholders of 15.6 per cent against 11.2 per cent. 'Founding-Family Ownership and Firm Performance: Evidence from the S&P 500', published in the *Journal of Finance*, drew similar conclusions.

Why do family businesses do so well? Family members often know the business inside out having grown up working in it. Decision making in family firms is usually quicker than in publicly quoted counterparts. A paternalist approach engenders loyalty in employees. Family firms are probably some of the few places left in the modern business world where the notion of a job for life isn't meaningless.

Family-firm owners usually have significant stock holdings in their companies. Family firms reinvest in the business to a greater extent than non-family businesses. There is also a board of directors packed with family members – an anathema to fans of corporate governance codes, but family members often assume a stewardship role because of their family ties to the company, in a way that other directors never could.

Despite the oft-quoted saying 'shirtsleeves to shirtsleeves in three generations', some family firms have managed substantially more than their allotted time. One of the world's oldest family businesses is the Japanese firm Kongo Gumi. Founded in 576, the construction company is on to the 40th generation. Not that far behind is Fonderia Pontificia Marinelli, an Italian company founded around the turn of the century – the 11th century. The company operates a bell foundry, and its bells toll from churches across the globe. Several of the firm's employees are from the Marinelli family.

72.   Can you fiddle your expenses?

If there is a system, then it is open to abuse. Business expenses are no exception. Claiming for things which aren't related to your job could tarnish your image within the company or even get you fired. Yet, despite the risks, many employees admit to submitting inaccurate business expenses at least once in their working lifetime.

A survey conducted by Onepoll.com for the hotel group Travel Lodge suggested that employees cost British companies £1 billion each year by fiddling their expenses. Of those who took part in the survey, 46 per cent believed it was a justifiable way to boost their income, and 8 per cent said that they were more likely to do it if their boss was annoying them at the time; only 4 per cent said that they had been caught. The average worker pockets an extra £14.60 every time they claim.

You might expect to find the occasional dubious claim for personal travel or entertainment, but there are those who like to push the boundaries of the legitimate business expense. Some of the more unlikely claims uncovered by the research were:

- Hamster for son's birthday present
- Pregnancy kit for a one night stand
- Masonic door knocker
- Collectable stamps for personal collection
- Dancing lessons
- Gucci watch
- New furniture for the house
- Condoms
- Neutering a cat

Women came out of the survey better than men, with 27 per cent of men claiming more than they are legitimately entitled to, compared to just 18 per cent of women.

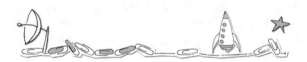

73. Is anything as safe as houses?

As many people know to their cost, there is no such thing as a 100 per cent safe investment. Companies fail, banks go bankrupt, commodity prices slump. The Wall Street Crash is a good example of the perils of investment.

In August 1921, the Dow Jones Industrial Average was 63.9. There followed a period of economic boom during which the optimism of a new technological age – with radio, cinema, the car, telephone, and aviation – drove stock prices to new records, and the Dow to a peak of 381.17 in September 1929.

In October 1929, however, the market turned, the Dow fell 38 points on Black Monday, and the mass selling that ensued overloaded the telephone and telegraph system. By July 1932, the Dow was down to 41.22. It would take over 20 years to recover. At the same time, the mass withdrawal of savings precipitated a banking crisis. The number of banks declined from 25,568 in 1929 to 14,771 in 1933.

Commodities are equally risky. The gold price has slumped more than once, as has the price of oil, as well as the value of other commodities like coffee, sugar, pork bellies and orange juice.

Another investment that is often touted as a sure-fire success is safe-as-houses property. For anyone who dismisses the 1989 UK property crash as a one-off blip, it is worth noting that, like any other asset class, property values go up and down according to supply and demand and other factors that affect the market.

The 1935 edition of Fortune business magazine contained an article about the boom city of the moment, Shanghai, 'the fifth city of the earth'. In 1843, explained Fortune, a few acres of land were set aside by treaty for foreigners, and the city opened to foreign trade. The land became known as the International Settlement or the Bund and, at the time, an acre could be bought for $500 (Mexican Eagle Dollars: 1935 value).

During the Taiping rebellion, which ran from 1850 to 1864 and was the second bloodiest war in human history, with estimated deaths of around 20 million, the Taiping army marched to the doors of Shanghai, sweeping a tide of refugees before it. However, the army did not take the Bund and, following the Taiping army's defeat, that acre of land could be sold for $50,000. By 1899, the city had become a bustling commercial centre, and the area of the Bund had increased four times since its creation.

Then, in 1912, the ruling Manchu dynasty collapsed, and the revolution under Sun Yat-Sen gave way to a period of unrest in China, with various warlords ruling different regions. The Chinese (and their savings) headed for Shanghai and, by 1924, the Chinese population was about three million on the Bund –and in 1927 property was selling there for $1,400,000 an acre. In 1935, following the Kuomintang revolution led by Chang Kai-Shek, that acre of land was worth $4,200,000.

Any property investor at this point might have been very happy with their return, had they invested in land in the International Settlement. Unfortunately, however, thousands were about to lose every penny they possessed. In 1937, the Japanese invaded Shanghai with scant regard for the property rights of foreign investors, or the sanctity of the International Settlement. The Second World War followed and, soon after, the final victory of the Communist party in China. So ended the safe-as-houses investment climate in Shanghai.

74. How do you ask for a bank loan?

In 1976, an enthusiastic young business woman wearing a Bob Dylan T-shirt asked for a £4000 bank loan to help her start a new business venture. She was turned down. Instead, her husband borrowed the money and gave it to her. Thirty years later, the business she founded was sold for £652 million. The entrepreneur was Anita Roddick, and the business The Body Shop.

Whether it's for personal use or for a business, asking for a bank for a loan can be a challenge. This is especially true if you haven't borrowed money before. With no track record, the bank is taking more of a risk lending the money. So how can you improve your chances of being accepted?

Don't be apprehensive. Lending money is what banks do. It is one of the main ways that they make their profits – so don't be shy. By doing your research, you will not only feel more confident but give yourself a better chance of success. Look for banks with loans that match your requirements. Make a list and rank them according to their different terms and conditions, in order of those that work best for you.

Before a meeting with your bank, ask what information they will need in order to approve your loan. Then make sure you take it with you, along with proof of who you are, what you need the money for and details of your financial background.

You will be asked why you need the loan, so prepare a brief presentation of what the loan is needed for and why you are a good risk. Questions that you are likely to be asked include: the amount needed; the duration of the loan; when and how you will repay the loan; and what you will do if you do not get the loan. Each of the responses you give to these questions will indicate to the bank how well you have thought out your needs, and therefore the level of risk you pose.

You are also more likely to be successful if you look and act in a professional manner. Dress appropriately, be positive and talk clearly.

Finally, provide facts not fiction. The bank employees will have sat through hundreds of loan application meetings, so it is no use trying to spin the facts. If the bank is able to see that you are aware of the potential pitfalls of your venture, they will be more inclined to approve your loan.

If you are rejected on your first attempt, it doesn't necessarily mean that other lenders will also reject you. Once you have secured and repaid a loan, the next time will be a whole lot easier.

75.   What happens when investors go mad?

In February 1720, shares in the South Sea Company, based in England, were trading at £130; by June, the price had shot up to an astonishing £1050. What followed was chaos, as the South Sea share bubble burst. By November 1720, the share price was back to £170. In the process, many fortunes were lost and many individuals were ruined. For anyone investing in the stock market, it is a cautionary tale showing how easy it is to get caught up in the investment equivalent of a goldrush.

According to classical finance theory, the disastrous rise and fall of the South Sea stock should never have happened in the first place. Efficient market hypothesis (EMH) states that prices in a market, at any given time, reflect all the information available. Don't believe you are buying or selling an under- or overpriced asset in a skilful attempt to make money.

But what if investor behaviour isn't quite as rational as the economists would like to believe? Behavioural finance is a new approach that attempts to explain events in financial and other markets by focusing on investor behaviour.

Academics at the Centre for Risk Research at the University of Southampton School of Management have identified a number of factors that determine whether people use information rationally. As excitement levels rise, so our ability to think in a rational manner decreases. Equally, as a problem becomes more complex, people hit a cognitive limit, and then the rational approach disappears.

That appears to be what happened in the South Sea bubble, and possibly in the dot com bubble, and the Black Monday stock market crash in 1987, where global markets slumped simultaneously.

The South Sea Company exchanged its shares for government debt. The company eventually converted half the British government's debt into tradeable securities.

Four share subscription offers were made to the public on credit: investors made an upfront payment, and paid the rest in instalments over a fixed period. Each issue involved a different down payment and instalment period.

A popular London lottery had just been run on a similar staged basis. There were five draws and each draw offered a larger prize. The public, stampeding to buy the stock, appeared to believe that, as with the lottery, each subscription issue would be more rewarding than the last. The whole venture – the pricing and structure of the subscriptions, the trading of the subscription receipts – was extremely complex.

No wonder the normal rules of the market didn't seem to apply. A lawyer at the time described the situation 'as if all the lunatics had escaped out of the madhouse at once'.

'I can calculate the motions of the heavenly bodies but not the madness of people,' observed Sir Isaac Newton, who lost money amid the feverish speculation.

76.   Hacked off?

In February of 2000, many of the most important online companies in the US, such as eBay, Yahoo and Amazon, suffered a technical glitch called Denial of Service, which caused a total of $1.7 billion in losses. The culprit turned out to be a 16-year-old Canadian responding to the alias 'Mafia Boy', who was caught after bragging to his friends about his deeds.

While the majority of people are trying to accumulate as much wealth as they can, there is a select group of people who take pleasure in wiping away other people's gains. Hackers, crackers and phreakers are people who either use computers to gain unauthorised access to data of some form or another or simply destroy a system's ability to function.

The practice of hacking dates back to the early 1960s at the Massachusetts Institute of Technology (MIT), where students tried to develop programmes of ever-greater complexity. A kind of geek one-upmanship. Mafia Boy was a cracker – a subset of the hacking fraternity. Crackers are the ones who wreak the most havoc. They specialise in causing damage, stealing information, deactivating software protection, entering restricted security areas and producing programming viruses.

Phreakers, such as Kevin Poulsen, hack telephone systems to make free long-distance phonecalls at someone else's expense and, in more extreme cases, break into the telephone systems of larger organisations to see what mischief they can get up to. Poulsen took over the Los Angeles phone lines in 1990. A radio station was offering a Porsche as a prize for whoever managed to be caller number 102. Surprise, surprise, it was Kevin Poulsen.

Perhaps the most famous hacker is Kevin Mitnik. Mitnik was on the run from the FBI for almost two years before being caught and serving a five-year prison sentence for infiltrating computer systems. These days, he has a poacher-turned-gamekeeper lifestyle as he advises multinational companies on how to keep people like himself out of their systems.

Regardless of attempts of governments to close down the unauthorised, illegal activities of some hackers, there will always be hacking, cracking, phreaking and whatever other variations are invented in the future. In many cases, for the perpetrators it is not about stealing money or maliciously doing damage, but more to do with the challenge of keeping one step ahead of security technology, curiosity, and a kind of Mount Everest 'because it was there' mentality.

Gary McKinnon, also known as Solo, allegedly hacked into over 90 computer systems including US Military systems, NASA, the Pentagon and a number of private companies. When asked by the *Guardian* what was the most exciting thing he saw while looking through the computer systems of the world's superpower, he said: 'A list of officers' names under the heading "Non-Terrestrial Officers". I found a list of "fleet-to-fleet transfers", and a list of ship names. I looked them up. They weren't US navy ships. What I saw made me believe they have some kind of spaceship, off-planet.'

77.   Is everyone to blame?

In an increasing litigious world, filing a lawsuit against someone is seen by many as the quickest and easiest way to get rich quick. Even if, in the eyes of many, it may look like you are the one at fault, there is still a chance that someone will pay out a small fortune for your misfortune.

In 1996, Robert Lee Brock, in a novel approach to litigation, tried to sue himself. At the time, Brock, a Virginia prison inmate, was no stranger to the courts, having lodged 29 appeals in 1995–96 alone. Brock complained about all aspects of his legal treatment and prison conditions including food, clothing, access to and the poor condition of the prison's law library, mail delivery, hot water, improper placement of a mirror for the disabled, phones, canteen needs, art supplies, mental stress and the price of coffee.

Finally, he sued himself. He claimed his civil rights and religious beliefs were violated when he allowed himself to get drunk. He demanded $5 million from himself. Rather cunningly though, as he didn't earn an income behind bars, he felt the state should pay. The case was thrown out.

While Brock was still languishing in his cell, Paul Shimkonis was out on the town, enjoying his bachelor party. One night in September 1996, Shimkonis and friends were enjoying the sights at Diamond Dolls, a strip bar in Florida. As the guest of honour, Shimkonis was asked to sit back on a low chair while one of the girls, Tawny Peaks (since retired), entertained him. During the ensuing lap dance, Peak's not-insubstantial breasts – 60 HH – were flung in Shimkonis' face. Some might consider this one of the highlights of the evening. Not Shimkonis though.

Shimkonis put in a claim for the amount of $15,000, claiming damages for whiplash, physical harm, disfigurement and mental anguish from the effects of the dancer's large breasts hitting him – he claimed they felt like 'cement blocks'. The parties agreed to take the matter to *The People's Court* TV show, and Shimkonis had his claim denied.

78.   What is the worst-paid job in the world?

You know what it feels like to be undervalued and underpaid, but is there someone, somewhere, worse off than you? The answer is almost definitely yes. Unless, that is, you are a tanzanite miner.

These miners stand on a ladder all day passing bags of loose rock from the miner below them to the miner above. They are not fed, and there are no breaks.

Sometimes, rival mining firms will dynamite a section and blow through into a competitor's mineshaft. When a natural disaster strikes (in one incident more than 100 were killed by flooding), many believe the local superstition that it is a ritual sacrifice and signifies a coming period of boom.

The people who undertake this type of work do so as a last, desperate option to escape poverty. So what do they get paid? Answer: in some cases, absolutely nothing. The mine owners expect the miners to steal, so they don't pay them. But the chances of getting a gem as it passes you on its journey towards the sky, mixed within bags of rock? Very slim indeed.

Section 6: Happiness and health

- What is the worst job in the world?
- When is it a good time to take a sickie?
- How much sleep do you need?
- What are the odds of getting shot at work?
- Should you cycle to work?
- Fancy spending some time at work doing your own thing?
- Which inventor has done the most damage to the world?
- Is business just a game to you?
- Does money make you sad?
- What's the best excuse for being late?
- Do you work too much?
- Is too much information bad for your health?
- Does your company make you happy?
- Are you burnt out?

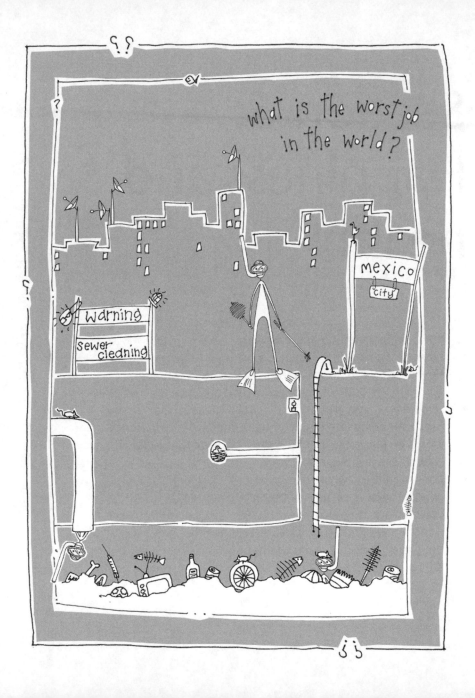

79. What is the worst job in the world?

Most people go through moments of hating their job. But, on those days when the world is against you, your boss is on your case and you still haven't finished that report that was due in a week ago, spare a thought for the people who do some of the unquestionably worst jobs in the world.

- *Professional dog-food taster.* Responsible for testing the consistency, texture and, of course, taste of dog food.
- *Clean-up team member, No. 4 reactor of the Chernobyl nuclear power station.* Previous experience not necessary. Career prospects – limited?

Admittedly, what one person considers unbearable, others spend many happy years doing. Pet-food tasting and nuclear waste disposal might be high up the career list for someone. As for the very worst of the worst, however, we think this deserves the prize.

- *Sewage Diver, Mexico City.* Job description: diving into raw sewage to remove blockages from the system including, quite frequently, dead bodies. Risks: getting one of numerous infections, being impaled by used syringes, drowning in raw sewage. Monthly pay: £400. Don't all rush at once.

80. When is it a good time to take a sickie?

According to management researchers, the first Monday in February is the most popular day of the year to take a day's unauthorised absence – a sickie. According to one employee survey, post-Christmas blues, poor weather and a big break before the next bank holiday combine to encourage 10 per cent of employees to take a sly day off. There is also the fact that staying away on Monday can help create enough days off in a row to make that long-weekend holiday worthwhile.

In the research, conducted by Cary Cooper, Professor of Organisational Psychology and Health at Lancaster University Management School, almost 20 per cent of those surveyed said that it was acceptable to text in sick, while 28 per cent owned up to faking coughs and splutters when phoning in.

While only 5 per cent admitted being caught out pulling a sickie, it is worth considering the possibility when deciding how to spend the day. During the 2006 Football World Cup, some businesses had so many employees calling in sick that they employed nurses to field the calls, check the symptoms and determine if people were faking it.

One company in the Lothians even went so far as to hire private detectives to catch two employees suspected of taking a sickie to watch the World Cup. The detectives launched a surveillance operation, following them from their homes until they met up in a West Lothian pub. Camera footage of their movements was then handed over to the firm.

According to figures published by the Confederation for British Industry, workers took an average of seven days off sick in 2006, compared with 6.6 days in 2005. The CBI estimated the cost to the economy at £13.4 billion, for a total of 175 million lost working days.

Alternatively, if you are fond of the odd day off but don't want to run the risk of disciplinary procedures, you could emigrate to a more enlightened country.

In some countries, you can take a sickie without fear of recrimination. Many companies in Sweden, for example, offer a number of 'mental health' days where employees can choose to take a day off whenever they feel like it. No need even for any fake coughing or spluttering.

81. How much sleep do you need?

No matter what you do in your job, a good amount of quality sleep the night before enables you to work better. But if you do choose to lose valuable hours of precious sleep by surfing the net into the early hours, does it really matter? Well, that probably depends on what your job is. There are some jobs where a drop in performance can have disastrous effects.

For example, if your job involves driving, here are some sobering statistics. Nearly 45,000 Britons die or are seriously injured in road accidents every year, and road safety experts say driver fatigue is a major cause. It is estimated to be responsible for a fifth of all accidents on motorways and trunk routes.

That's why tachographs have been used since the 1950s, to regulate the number of hours commercial drivers do each day, although these have been subject to tampering, and electronic versions are being implemented in a further attempt to reduce road accidents.

Adequate sleep is essential not only for a productive day and the immediate safety of those around you, but also for your own long-term health. If we are deprived of sleep, we are more likely to suffer heart attacks, get diabetes and be paranoid. The *Wall Street Journal* reported that $70 billion is lost per year in productivity, accidents, and health costs as a result of workers' inability to adjust to late-night work schedules.

It is estimated that adults need between seven and eight hours sleep per night on average. In the UK, the Sleep Research Centre at Loughborough puts the figure a little more conservatively at not less than six hours. Albert Einstein needed more than nine hours of sleep, Margaret Thatcher around four.

If, after reading this, you feel like taking a nap, spare a thought for the company directors who are the most sleep-deprived of all, averaging 5.9 hours a night, with a weary 8 per cent getting under four hours of rest per night.

If you need a good night's rest, PR or marketing might be the best bet. Travelodge's 2007 sleep study found that, of those who said they got enough sleep, a more restful 86 per cent were employed in these functions, although that might only be because 95 per cent of them said they fall asleep on the sofa once they get home from work.

82.   What are the odds of getting shot at work?

Workplace violence is a significant problem in business life. Especially in the US, it seems. In July 2003, an employee at a Lockheed Martin plant in Meridian, Mississippi, shot 14 co-workers, killing six. In August 2003, a disgruntled ex-employee gunned down and killed six people at an auto-parts warehouse in Chicago. In April 2007, a worker at NASA's Johnson Space Centre in Houston shot his supervisor. The list goes on.

According to US Department of Labor statistics, there were 564 workplace homicides in the US in 2005 – an increase from 559 in 2004. The workers at most risk were barbers and other 'personal appearance' workers, with 100 victims. It is not clear if this was in response to the quality of their work. Second on the most-likely-to-be-murdered-at-work list came food and beverage servers (77).

In the UK, the workers most likely to be the victims of an assault are, unsurprisingly, people engaged in the protective service occupations. But next come managers and proprietors in agriculture and services. The likelihood of being a victim of at least one violent incident, threat or assault was estimated at 1500 per 100,000 workers per year.

In the US, the Occupational Safety and Health Administration (OSHA) defines workplace violence as 'violence or the threat of violence against workers'. That includes verbal assaults as well as physical violence. OSHA estimates that two million Americans are the victims of workplace violence each year.

According to the Bureau of Labor Statistics, 95 per cent of the 7.1 million US employers reported at least one act of some type of workplace violence in 2006. Worryingly, about 43 per cent of those threatened and 24 per cent of those attacked at work don't report the incident.

83.   Should you cycle to work?

Every so often, there is a campaign to improve the nation's health. Usually, as part of that campaign, the public is urged to get off the tube a station early, and walk the rest of the way. We should, it is suggested, walk to work instead of driving or getting the bus. Run up a flight of stairs instead of taking the lift. And then there is that staple of the national fitness campaign – the call to cycle.

Cycling to work is healthy and fun, according to the London Cycling Campaign. There is a tax-exempt loan scheme for cycle purchase that companies can implement. According to Transport for London, regular cyclists tend to be fitter and healthier than non-cyclists. Cycling England estimates that 600,000 people already cycle to work.

So why wouldn't you cycle to work if you could? A quick look at the Royal Society for the Prevention of Accidents figures puts a spoke in the wheel of the cycling lobby. Each year, some 16,000 people are killed or injured while riding a bicycle; of those, 2100 are killed or seriously injured. That's just the injuries that are reported. Between 60 to 90 per cent of cyclist casualties are not reported.

In the cities there are all those cars and people to avoid, plus the bendy buses, normal buses and trams, not forgetting the millions of potholes and road blemishes that could tip you over at any moment. According to one article published in *The American Journal of Public Health*, per kilometre travelled, a cyclist in America is 12 times likelier than a car occupant to be killed.

So next time you are tempted to improve your health by jumping on the back of the cycling peloton, consider the evidence first before trading your bus pass for a crash helmet.

84.   Fancy spending some time at work doing your own thing?

Why spend all your time at work doing your job? Why not use part of your working day to pursue your own projects, let your creativity run free and work up some new business ideas?

In most companies, slacking off the usual responsibilities would earn a reprimand and eventually, if continued, dismissal. But at some companies such activity is encouraged and even rewarded.

Google, the search company based in Mountain View, California, likes its employees to unleash the entrepreneurial spirit within, allowing staff 20 per cent of their time to spend working on whatever they want to – aside from the organisation's core business.

The resulting start-ups within the company are known as Googlettes, and many become an important element of Google's mainstream business. Orkut, the social networking website, is an example of a grown-up Googlette.

Another American champion of the 'let the employees have some free time during work' concept is 3M, the diversified tech company based in St. Paul, Minnesota. Former CEO William McKnight is widely credited with introducing a number of organisational policies that allow individuals the freedom to innovate within organisational boundaries, unfettered to a degree by the hierarchical control.

3M's techniques aimed at encouraging employee innovation include the 15 per cent option, where some employees are able to spend 15 per cent of their time pursuing the projects they want to. They just get on with it, without any obligation to tell managers or justify what they are doing. Workers who want to work on their own ideas during 3M working time can bid for funding from business unit managers or, if unsuccessful, apply for an internal grant.

It is innovation policies like these that have made Google one of the fastest growing brands, by value, in the world, and have helped produce a string of innovative products at 3M, including Scotch tape and Post-It notes.

85. Which inventor has done the most damage to the world?

Perhaps innovation is going to be the secret to your success. You might have an idea that will revolutionise the way people live or travel. Thomas Midgley Jr was a mechanical engineer who later turned to chemistry and managed to do both.

For his ingenuity, he was awarded several honours including the William H. Nichols medal from the American Chemical Society in 1922, the Perkins Medal in 1937, the Priestley Medal in 1941 and the William Gibbs Medal in 1942.

So what world enhancing developments did this legend of chemistry create? Well, among over a hundred different patents, he created leaded fuel and the use of CFCs in refrigerators and aerosols.

Today we see them as harmful to the environment, the former causing billions of tonnes of lead to be pumped into the atmosphere, causing a variety of health problems around the world, and the latter responsible for the hole in the ozone layer, but at the time they were seen as technological developments.

Midgley realised that, if tetra-ethyl lead was added to petrol, the fuel would burn in a more controlled manner, thereby allowing the engines to run more smoothly. In a smart marketing move, General Motors, the company he worked for, named the new substance 'Ethyl' and avoided mentioning the lead content.

The discovery of dichlorodifluoromethane, a chlorinated fluorocarbon or CFC, by Midgley occurred when General Motors asked him to find a safe alternative to the toxic and flammable substances that were used in the 1920s to run refrigerators and other household appliances. He called it 'Freon' and it was also later used as the propellant in aerosol cans and inhalers. It was years before scientists began to understand what these two inventions were doing to the environment.

Midgley never stopped inventing. After he contracted polio and was left severely disabled, he devised a system of pulleys to lift him from his bed. Unfortunately, it turned out that even this invention was flawed because, at the age of 55, he became entangled in it and died of strangulation.

So it seems that, even when you have the best of intentions, you can still cause a whole lot of trouble for yourself and the world in general.

86. Is business just a game to you?

Why leave work at the office when you can bring it home? You can even incorporate it into your family leisure time, by playing a business-related board game.

Trading games are particularly popular, and there are scores to choose from. You can, for example, take a step back in time to the days when the despotic Medici family were a dominant force in Europe, and exert your iron-trading grip on the continent. Other trading games cover the Silk Road, pre-World War I Europe and Ancient Greece.

Alternatively, you could get into the energy business with *Power Grid*, the real estate business with *Fifth Avenue*, the railroad business with *Railroad Tycoon* or farming with *Hacienda*. Megalomaniacs might prefer *I'm the Boss*, and to get down to some tough negotiating.

There are business-trading games played with cards, too. *Business* was published in 1903, with players trading their cards to corner the railway stock market. In the similar, but better-known, *Pit*, published by Parker Brothers in 1904, players corner the market in a particular type of commodity.

Possibly the most famous business game of all is *Monopoly*®. The game has its origins in a number of variants which were developed in the 1930s, and which date back to *The Landlord's Game*, created by Elizabeth Magie in 1904, which was designed to show how a single tax could work. *Monopoly*, the most popular commercial board game in the world, was patented in 1935 by Charles Darrow in the US and released by Parker Brothers.

87.   Does money make you sad?

It seems the Beatles were on to something when they wrote 'money can't buy you love'. Research from social scientists and psychologists suggests that, despite average income levels continuing to increase in developed economies, happiness levels are moving in the opposite direction.

While wealthier countries do tend to be happier than poor nations, once a person has certain essentials, and average incomes reach £10,000 a year, extra income doesn't appear to make much difference to overall happiness. In fact, people in the UK are much less happy today than they were in the 1950s, despite being three times wealthier.

This is worrying, given that many people place happiness as more important to their lives than money. There is also evidence to suggest that happy people live longer than those who are miserable. The difference can be almost ten years, according to some studies.

No wonder some countries take happiness very seriously. Take the example of the Kingdom of Bhutan, a small country located in the Himalaya mountain range, wedged between India and China, with a population of about 600,000.

When the country was criticised for making slow economic progress, Bhutan's King replied that Gross National Happiness was more important than Gross National Product.

Unfortunately, data from other happiness surveys, such as that of the Netherlands-based World Happiness Institute or the World Values Institute in Stockholm, suggests that the world is fairly miserable place. The University of Leicester in the UK has produced a world happiness map, or, as it prefers to call it, a global projection of subjective wellbeing.

The top five happiest nations are: Denmark; Switzerland; Austria; Iceland; and the Bahamas. Bhutan is ranked number eight. The UK languishes well down the list at 41. There is little sign of *joie de vivre* with the stereotypically miserable French shrugging their collective shoulders at 62. And the Japanese are outstandingly unhappy as a nation at 90.

88.   What's the best excuse for being late?

Struggled to get in to work because the wind was blowing against you? Leaves on the line? Held up by that mountain lion in the road? These are just a few of the excuses that employees have offered for turning up late for work. If only this kind of creative effort was put into their working day, who knows what might be achieved.

Here are a few other prize-winning examples of this type of literary fiction:

'When I got up this morning I took two Ex-Lax thinking they were vitamin pills';

'I had a row with my girlfriend and she shredded all my clothes'; and

'I was putting moisturiser on my face a bit too vigorously and gave myself a nosebleed.'

If tardiness is something you suffer from, then you have probably had to deliver an excuse or several to your boss for being late to work. If, however, you are short on invention, or fresh out of excuses, we offer our own mini how-to guide.

Option 1: it's so unbelievable it must be true

This is the preferred option for creative types. You need to be very convincing to pull this one off. Either it needs to actually be true or you will need to be a good actor. An example may look like this:

'When I woke up this morning at my usual time of 6:15 am, I discovered that my dog had eaten my computer's memory stick, on which I had saved the report you had requested. I had to choose between rewriting it and waiting for it to pass through my dog before I came into work. I opted to rewrite and that's why I am late.'

Option 2: brutal honesty

These are the kind of excuses you might start giving when you are already looking for somewhere else to work. You may have an understanding manager who helps you through the issues you present them with, but it's more likely you will get a warning and eventually be fired. Here are a couple of one-liners that may do the trick:

'I just wasn't in the right frame of mind this morning and work is so passé'; or

'My team are driving me insane so I came in late.'

Option 3: honesty backed with commitment

This is the one that is most likely to keep you in your job. It is an admission that a mistake was made and that you will not let it happen again. For example:

'My alarm clock didn't work this morning. I will buy a new one so it doesn't happen again'; or

Or 'I missed my train connection. I will give myself more time in future.'

Option 4: you are losing it, and arguing with you will only make things worse

This can be difficult to pull off and is not without risk; after all, you don't want to be sectioned for the sake of a few extra minutes in bed. Delivered with eyes staring into space, this may have the desired affect:

'I woke up and thought I was temporarily deaf.'

When all is said and done, will your excuse get you off the hook? A survey conducted by CareerBuilder.com found that 27 per cent of HR professionals seriously doubt most of the excuses people give and, as the saying goes, when it comes to excuses, your friends don't need them and your enemies won't believe them.

89. Do you work too much?

'I personally work long hours, but not as long as I used to,' Bill Gates once observed. 'I certainly haven't expected other people to work as hard as I did. Most days I don't work more than 12 hours. On weekends I rarely work more than eight hours. There are weekends I take off and I take vacations.'

For many people, increasingly long hours are an unfortunate reality. The International Labour Organisation (ILO) conducts a number of studies on working hours. In 2006, it concluded that one in five workers around the world – over 600 million people – work 'excessively' long hours.

Long working hours are defined by the ILO as over 48 hours a week. In the ILO study, which covered 50 countries, over a quarter of the UK working population put in over 48 hours a week, compared to 19 per cent in Switzerland and 18 per cent in the US.

There is a well-documented link between long working hours and poor health. A study by the UK's Institute of Management and the University of Manchester Institute of Science and Technology revealed that the ideal of a well-balanced work and home life was some way off. Over 80 per cent of executives worked over 40 hours a week; one in ten worked over 60 hours. Depressingly, 86 per cent said that the long hours had an effect on their relationship with their children and 71 per cent said that it damaged their health.

If you think workers in the UK have it tough, spare a thought for millions toiling away in the emerging economies. Half of the workforce in Peru turns in a

48-plus-hour week, as do 49.5 per cent of the Korean workforce and 46 per cent of workers in Thailand. Not so much work-life balance, as work-work balance.

90.   Is too much information bad for your health?

We live in an age where we are bombarded by a barrage of information, from a myriad of sources – internet, email, mobile phones, satellite television – as part of an always-on existence that impairs our performance at work and our ability to relax at home.

It's all part of a phenomenon tagged information overload. Worryingly, information overload is not just bad for your performance at work; it's bad for your health. A study by Hewlett Packard revealed that some people are becoming addicted to email and text messages (BlackBerry users, see Question 17). The guilty workers exhibited a number of traits: they checked work messages at home or on holiday (62 per cent); they always responded to an email immediately or as soon as possible (over 50 per cent); and they admitted that they would interrupt a meeting to respond to an email (21 per cent).

This 'infomania' is bad for your brain – it makes you more stupid (or less clever, if you prefer). Dr Glenn Wilson, the University of London psychologist, carried out a study at the Institute of Psychiatry, which found that excessive use of technology reduces workers' intelligence.

The infomaniacs, distracted by incoming email and phone calls, showed a ten point fall in IQ test performance – twice that found in studies of the impact of smoking marijuana. Anyone who needs a good eight hours' sleep should also beware: constantly breaking away from tasks to react to email or text messages causes similar effects on the mind as losing a night's sleep.

91.   Does your company make you happy?

Happiness is an important thing to have in the workplace, and many organisations acknowledge this in their efforts to increase their employees' happiness quotient. Some companies may provide free car parking for their employees; others have subsidised cafeterias, childcare or gym membership.

Some organisations, however, are a little more creative in the drive for a happy workforce. UBS, the investment banking and securities firm, has a clear commitment to the sponsoring of various arts projects, including several orchestras. Not unusual, you say. Well, UBS has gone much further by offering its employees a choral society, an orchestra and subsidised music lessons. There's even a piano for them to play in one meeting room. As Edward Kay, a UBS employee and music club committee member, stated in an interview with *The Times*: 'I couldn't have pursued music in such an active way if it was not for work.'

The whole notion of work-life balance means that many more businesses are helping their staff to spend quality time with their families. Services can include childcare leave, adoption assistance, working time flexibility for employees and family days.

The focus on happy employees has moved so far up the agenda that even the developers of business parks are planning and building facilities that will make life easier and happier for all who work there. When Chiswick Park, a business park in south-west London, was developed, they didn't just focus on the spaces people would use when working, but they also built a gym and a swimming pool. Beyond that, they also offer evening classes, ranging from sailing to creative writing.

Companies are now also more likely to let you go off on a sabbatical than they have ever been. Websites like gapyear.com are as likely to cater for the professional taking a break as they are for the recently graduated student.

Senior executives take sabbaticals too. In 1992, Ben Cohen, co-founder of Ben & Jerry's, took a six-month sabbatical. Although he didn't spend it travelling around the world or visiting exotic locations. Instead, he learnt to weld – so he could make a mailbox for co-founder Jerry Greenfield.

92.   Are you burnt out?

If you live in Peru, the answer is very likely to be yes, judging by the ILO figures. But burnout is not confined to emerging economies by any means.

Outsourcing and other cost-cutting measures mean that many companies have fewer people working harder and for longer. In Japan, for example, death by overwork has a specific name –karoshi.

Karoshi was a significant social problem in Japan during the late 1980s. The country's economic miracle ground to a halt, the number of hours put in by workers increased and unemployment became a growing concern. The social stigma attached to redundancy meant that overworked salarymen, who had been used to the idea of a job for life, were often unwilling to complain even when their workload became unbearable.

In June 2000, Dentsu, the Japanese advertising company, made legal history by admitting responsibility for the karoshi of an employee who committed suicide in 1991. Ichori Oshima worked an average of 80 hours a week, on gruelling shifts that sometimes lasted from 9 am to 6 am the following morning. The case against Oshima's employer was pursued by his parents for eight years. The company belatedly demonstrated its remorse to the tune of Y168 million ($1.65 million). For Oshima, it was too late.

The Japanese government began compiling annual karoshi statistics in 2003, using the application and awards of workers' compensation to family members as a basis. In 2003, 158 deaths were attributed to overwork. In 2006, 355 workers fell severely ill or died from overwork in the year to March. This was the highest figure since the government began keeping records. As well as karoshi victims, 819 workers claimed that they became mentally ill due to overwork, with 205 applicants awarded compensation.

Section 7: Department of miscellany

- Is it worth aggravating so many people with junk mail?
- Does anything ever get built on time and under budget?
- What's Shakespeare got to do with it?
- Can you face the music?
- What is a coolhunter?
- What happened to the paperless office?
- Are you on the same page?
- What happens when re-branding goes wrong?
- How competitive is the UK?
- Is the demographic time bomb dangerous?
- Is Chinese the business language of the future?
- Are you feeling guilty?
- Are you talking about the Y Generation?
- Do you know a good slogan when you hear one?
- What is scenario planning?
- Why should I care about Web 2.0?
- Does something smell fishy?
- What is the most valuable brand?
- Is your mission impossible?
- Do Skunk Works work?

93. Is it worth aggravating so many people with junk mail?

Believe it or not, direct marketing has been around for almost 500 years. Ever since moveable type was invented (around 1450), people have been producing catalogues and touting them around.

Direct marketing drives purchases, using a variety of media, by instigating a specific call to action. For example: 'DIY your home by calling 0800 SUPER DRILL.'

In recent years, the use of the internet in direct marketing has greatly increased, with spamming – bulk emailing – becoming the scourge of many email account-holders. However, direct marketing is still predominantly associated with the production and distribution of junk mail.

In terms of junk mail's popularity today, it seems that you can broadly split society into two groups: those who produce it and love it and those who receive it and hate it.

In the book *50 Simple Things You Can Do To Save The Earth*, stopping unwanted junk mail came in at number two – and it's not surprising when you review some of the statistics.

- Each year, 100 million trees are used to produce junk mail.
- 250,000 homes could be heated with one day's supply of junk mail.
- Americans receive almost 4 million tons of junk mail every year.
- In the UK, 5.4 billion direct mail items were sent through the post in 2004, and an additional 15 billion inserts and door-to-door promotions were produced.

The marketers get your name and address by buying lists and databases that contain your information. Every time you sign up to a loyalty card, apply for a credit card or return a product warrantee slip, your information is stored on a database. This valuable information, which you have willingly given, is then sold on to companies hungry for your business.

Eliminating it altogether is difficult, but there are a couple ways to reduce it. Firstly, don't give away your information unless it is absolutely necessary, and always tick the 'do not pass on my information' box when filling in forms. You can also call all the companies you have a legitimate association with and be asked to be removed from lists that may be sold on to third parties.

Perhaps the most efficient way to reduce the junk in the UK is to sign up to the mail preference service, which stops around 95 per cent of direct mail. A final indication of just how unpopular direct marketing is comes from America. In 2003, a 'National-do-not-call' registry was created, which in one year saw 62 million people sign up.

94. Does anything ever get built on time and under budget?

Every industry has it at some time or another – project completion delay and the associated increase in costs. For whatever reason, things just don't seem to stay on plan and costs begin to mount.

In construction, building sometimes commences before designs are 100 per cent complete, or the designs are complete, but then modified later on. In 1985,

Indiana's PSI Energy was forced to write off $2.7 billion in construction costs for a half-built nuclear reactor.

In 1970, the projected cost to construct the Montreal Olympic Stadium was $134 million (Canadian Dollars). However, delays to construction (mostly due to strikes) caused this to escalate to $264 million by the time it opened. Even then, the building was not yet complete, with the roof and tower being added later. It took over another 30 years before it was finally paid for in full. The final bill in 2006, including running repairs, interest and inflation, came to $1.61 billion. No wonder Quebecers call the stadium the Big Owe.

This is not uncommon. The Sydney Opera House went 1400 per cent over budget and the production of the supersonic passenger plane Concorde went over by 1100 per cent.

The IT industry has a variety of phrases to describe the conditions that lead to budgets being wildly underestimated and projects overrunning. Scope creep, requirement creep and feature creep all describe uncontrolled changes to the projects parameters. This can occur when a project is not clearly defined or controlled: new products and features are developed before the original project is completed, and the desire to include them leads to a loss of focus and an overshooting of budget and schedule. When this gets completely out of control, it is sometimes referred to as 'kitchen sink syndrome' – a desire to include absolutely everything in a project.

The National Programme for IT is a 10-year programme that aims to give 50 million patients in England an electronic health record. It is hailed by the NHS as the 'world's biggest civil information technology programme'. With an initial budget of £6.2 billion, it seems likely that the final figure will be between three and five times as much.

There are those who say that, if you deliver on time and on budget, then the challenge wasn't great enough – but try telling that to the Bechtel Corporation.

Bechtel had an immense challenge ahead of it when it started the construction of the Hoover Dam in 1931 during the dark days of the depression. At the time, it was the largest civil engineering project in the history of the United States and, even by today's standards, it boasts some incredible statistics: 3.7 million cubic yards of rock were excavated; 45 million pounds of pipe and structural steel were erected; and 4.4 million cubic yards of concrete were poured. The Hoover Dam stands at a height of 726 feet, is 1200 feet across the crest, and 660 feet thick at its base. Yet, remarkably, the entire project was completed under budget and two years ahead of schedule.

95.   What's Shakespeare got to do with it?

Management commentators have looked in some strange places for leadership icons. Alongside the usual suspects – military heroes, statesman and monarchs, people such as Napoleon, Wellington, Elizabeth I and Churchill – are more unusual sources of inspiration.

Take *Power Plays: Shakespeare's Lessons in Leadership and Management* by John Whitney, a professor at Columbia Business School in New York, and theatrical director Tina Packer. Or Shakespeare on Management: Leadership Lessons for Managers by Paul Corrigan. The Bard is big in business.

In *Power Plays,* for example, the authors argue that the real tragedy of Othello is that his human resource management skills weren't quite up to scratch. Every time you appoint someone to a job, someone else who thinks they should have got the job gets overlooked. In Othello's case, Iago was bypassed and subsequently wreaked havoc in his quest for vengeance.

But why stop at Shakespeare? At the management-goes-to-the-movies website www.moviesforbusiness.com, executives can take inspiration from Hollywood. As a sample of what the website has to offer, there is the case study of business lessons from *The Wizard of Oz*. Yes, you did read that correctly.

There are a number of business lessons to be learnt from the film version of Frank Baum's bestseller, including: 'Cowardly Lions Often Lead the Charge'; 'Don't Be a "Don't Bother Me" Boss'; and 'Become (Like the Professor) a Data-Sufficiency Expert'.

A good example is 'Learn to Mentor Like CEO Glinda', which starts thus: 'Consider the geo-politics of Oz. It's a world of contrast and conflict. There are pleasant, well-run countries in the North and South, presided over by benevolent queens (okay, good witches). The Munchkins live just within their borders, singing, dancing and frolicking beside the Yellow Brick Road. Then there are the Witchdoms of the East and West, ruled by evil sisters controlling armies of ape-like beings held in thrall.' And we thought the film was just a star vehicle for Judy Garland.

Other films you can draw on for business inspiration include *Moby Dick* (leadership), *Zulu* (leveraging resources), *Citizen Kane* (succession) and *Big* (creativity).

96. Can you face the music?

Existing customers, press 1. For sales, press 2. All other enquiries, press 3. You press 1 and get a telephone operator. No, of course you don't. You get on-hold music. Probably panpipe covers of songs, because research has shown that we hold on longer with this music playing in the background than when there is a looped, recorded message.

Listen carefully and you suddenly realise that music is everywhere in our lives, subtly manipulating our behaviour. Organisations wised up to the influence that sound can have over people ages ago. The US army used to play ghostly music to the Viet Cong during the Vietnam War, and it wasn't to cheer them up. Later, during the US invasion of Panama, the Vatican embassy was blasted with the dulcet tones of Welcome to the Jungle by Guns n' Roses, among other tunes. This was not because General Noriega, the ousted leader seeking refuge in the Vatican embassy, was a rock music fan, but in an effort to drive him out. (Although it has been said it was actually to keep bored US soldiers happy, or to hide negotiations from the media. But, having heard the track, we prefer the original theory.)

Music is a very powerful moderator of consumer behaviour, and there is all manner of research to support this. Although most consumers are unaware either of the research, or that they are being influenced. Not any longer though.

One study showed that playing slower in-store music slows supermarket shopping by 15 per cent, leading to a 33 per cent increase in spend. Also, fast music leads to fast drinking. So fast music in bars, slow music in shops, and classical music in wine merchants, where it leads to the purchase of more expensive wine.

Another study involved people being exposed to either silence or three different types of music: easy listening, pop or classical. They were asked how much they would pay for a list of 14 items. The results were as follows. Silence: £14.30. Easy listening: £14.51. Pop: £16.61. Classical: £17.23. Silence is not so golden.

Music even affects productivity. When 72 employees working in a NatWest Bank cheque-processing centre were exposed to no music, slow music or fast music over a three-week period, their productivity varied dramatically. With fast music, 23390.51 cheques were processed every half hour, but with slow music the figure was only 19129.17 – a 22 per cent increase. Cue hardcore techno in every office.

For those with an intense dislike of piped music, you are not alone. Pipe-down is a campaign against muzak, backed by, among others, the Royal National Institute of the Deaf.

97. What is a coolhunter?

You work hard and make all that money, but what are you going to spend it on, apart from food and the rent or mortgage? The trouble is, when you are busy working a 48-plus-hour week, answering emails, texts, mobile phone calls, and generally keeping your head above water, there is little time to keep up with the latest consumer trends.

Companies have the same problem: they need to anticipate consumer demand, but also have to spend time delivering and improving existing products and services.

Fortunately, there is a solution for time-poor employees and corporations. Since the beginning of the 1990s, a group of marketers has evolved, specialising in the detection of global consumer trends, before they even become trends. These coolhunters, as they are known, hang out in trendy urban areas, at colleges and bars, at holiday destinations ... anywhere that the hip 12–24 generation is likely to be found. They record consumer lifestyles and, using a variety of media, extrapolate trends and patterns as they emerge.

As a consumer, if you visit a coolhunters' website, like thecoolhunter.net or trendguide.com, you can find out about the very, very latest in fashion, gadgets and much more. Learn about the latest firewire speakers, lighting stripes, magic tape and velvet trainers. Discover the trendiest hotels and freshest destinations.

If you are going to spend your money, you might as well impress your colleagues with your unerring sense of style.

As for companies, if they are not doing so already, they would do well to browse through the coolhunter websites: these are the consumer markets of tomorrow, today.

98.   What happened to the paperless office?

In the late 1800s, Thomas Edison created the phonograph – as a dictation machine to replace paper memos, rather like the forerunner of the MP3 player. In 1975, an article in *Business Week* predicted that the office of the future would be almost devoid of paper. (Fold that sheet of A4 paper neatly into a paper plane and launch it across the office while waiting for paper's demise.)

In the late 1980s, Lars Kolind, then CEO of Danish hearing aid manufacturer Oticon, pronounced the death of paper in the workplace. Prematurely, as it turned out.

No more overstuffed filing cabinets, warehouses crammed with fading invoices, or paper trail, said Kolind. The future was a more efficient 'paperless office' – and Oticon would lead the way. The company even installed an interesting architectural feature: a shredder connected to a transparent chute which passed through the company cafeteria below, allowing workers to watch a satisfying stream of falling paper on its way to the recycling bins.

In the 1990s, legendary advertising boss Jay Chiat, of ad agency Chiat/Day, was inspired to create a virtual office. On top of eliminating personal office space, his plan involved ridding the office of paper. The results were not entirely in keeping with Chiat's vision. Employees stashed paper in their car boots, or towed it around the office in trolleys.

Today, paper retains its stubborn grip on office life. We use more paper in the workplace than ten years ago. It seems people are just wedded to the stuff, and for good reason, says Clive Holtham, Professor of Information Management at Cass Business School, City of London.

He draws a distinction between information work and knowledge work. Knowledge workers are either creating new knowledge or sharing it. 'Our research suggests that knowledge workers need paper for many knowledge tasks,' says Holtham.

'At the point that someone is doing their creative work, they should not be made to feel ashamed to be using paper; they should be encouraged to use it. People should go back to using paper; they might be more creative that way.'

Tech companies, on the other hand, never cease to proclaim the replacement for paper in the form of one electronic book or another. But what happens when you drop your e-book in the bath? Exactly.

99.   Are you on the same page?

Do you like to 'get your ducks in order' to enable some 'blue-sky thinking'? Or perhaps you are 'thinking outside the box' and 'having a brain dump'. If any of these are true, then you have welcomed management speak into your life –

and the chances are that you are baffling some people with it and aggravating others.

As the father of advertising, David Ogilvy, once said, 'Our business is infested with idiots who try to impress by using pretentious jargon.'

And it seems he is not alone in disliking the everyday use of jargon. In fact, a 2006 survey for Investors in People found that 54 per cent of employees in the UK regarded management jargon as a source of communication problems, and 37 per cent thought that it made people feel inadequate and resulted in mistrust in the workplace.

The same study showed that 39 per cent of people thought that the use of management jargon showed a lack of confidence. So if you are using it as part of your everyday language, be warned: a hefty 18 per cent think people who use jargon are untrustworthy and may be trying to cover something up.

However, there can be some light relief that comes out of a jargon-filled meeting – buzzword bingo. The game is very simple. Players make – or download – a bingo card, but rather than numbers, they use corporate jargon. Each card consists of 40 examples of current business buzzwords. Favourites include: out-of-the-box thinking; incentivise; the big picture; win-win; empower; touch base; square the circle; drill down; heads up; face time; and helicopter view.

At meetings, players tick off these phrases as they emerge from the lips of unsuspecting bosses. The first person to complete a row by ticking off five buzzwords is the winner.

So if in a meeting someone shouts 'House!' while you are pontificating, it's unlikely they are referring to the company's capital investment programme.

100. What happens when re-branding goes wrong?

The world may be full of brands of all types, shapes and sizes, but it is also cluttered with expensive brand disasters. Brands may be big and brash, but they are also delicate: even the most powerful brands need handling with care.

In the 1980s, Robert Goizueta became CEO at one of the great global brands: Coca-Cola. At the time, Coca-Cola was facing a tough challenge. Arch rival, Pepsi Co., had invented a brilliant marketing tactic: the 'Pepsi Challenge' taste test. In a blind taste test, many consumers preferred Pepsi to Coke.

Goizueta was prepared to take risks to boost the fortunes of Coca-Cola and, in April 1985, he announced that Coca-Cola was replacing its traditional recipe cola with New Coke. It was, according to Goizueta, 'the boldest single marketing move in the history of the consumer goods business.' Unfortunately, it was also one of the major marketing mistakes of the 20th century.

Yes, Pepsi was a threat, but the old version of Coke was still selling millions of units every day. Introducing New Coke made the existing Coca-Cola brand look weak. Not the behaviour of a market leader. Furthermore, producing a drink named 'New Coke' went against the brand values of tradition and authenticity. Traditional Coke had millions of loyal fans around the globe, and they reacted very angrily to the change, claiming the new formula tasted like furniture polish and sewer water.

In July, only 90 days after the launch of New Coke, the original coke was re-introduced as Classic Coke.

Coke might have been excused its mistake were it not for the fact that the dramatic effects of tinkering with a well-established, well-loved brand had already played out in the US drinks market a few years before.

In 1974, Schlitz was America's second most popular brand of beer. The company, founded in the 1850s, had 16.1 per cent of the American market and appeared secure in its position among the best-loved beers in the US. But then, the beer's brewers decided to tamper with the tried-and-tested formula and introduce a revolutionary new process – 'accelerated batch fermentation'. This saved time and money – a triumph for all concerned.

Unfortunately, the customers were not as enthusiastic as the company. They believed the beer was not up to the standards they had come to expect – it tasted the same, but customers believed it wasn't the same. Schlitz's market share fell to less than a single percentage point, and the value of its name declined from in excess of $1 billion in 1974 to around $75 million in 1980.

101. How competitive is the UK?

As in many other countries, the government in the UK is big on the idea that innovation is the route to greater productivity and competitiveness. Competitiveness is a tricky thing to measure. Fortunately, the World Economic Forum can help here. Each year the World Economic Forum produces its *Global Competitiveness Report*. So how is the UK faring against the rest of the world?

The good news is that the UK is comfortably ahead of Malta and Barbados, and even Italy and France. Not such good news is that, according to the World Economic Forum, the UK is still behind nine other nations, including the spectacularly competitive Nordic countries, including Sweden, Denmark, and Finland, and also other countries including the Netherlands, Germany – and the number one country, Switzerland. Plus, the UK slipped down a place between the 2005 and 2006 rankings.

Of course, no ranking is worth much if there isn't some competing ranking. True to ranking form, head over to IMD business school and you can catch the 2007 World Competitiveness Scoreboard, although UK policymakers may prefer to stick with the World Economic Forum's version.

Unfortunately for the UK, the IMD version of the global competitiveness league table doesn't make pleasant reading. Sure, the UK is still ahead of Italy, Greece, France and India. This time, though, the UK weighs in at No. 20, behind the usual array of Nordic countries, Finland, Denmark, Sweden, plus Norway and the closely related Iceland. Other countries that have stolen a competitive march on the UK include: New Zealand, China, Germany, and the top placed nation, the US.

So much for all those long hours we work, then.

102. Is the demographic time bomb dangerous?

There is a lot of conflicting evidence on the demographic future of the world. The demographic time bomb was a popular subject for magazine articles in the 1980s. As a generation of post-war baby boomers grew older, eventually they would become, as retirees, an unbearable burden on the generation that followed.

So demographic predictions suggested that, by 2000, there will be more US workers in their late 40s than in their late 20s, and that the number of 40- to 59-year-olds in the United States – 53 million in 1990 – will reach 83 million in 2010.

According to UN statistics in 2006, the fear of the demographic time bomb in North America was largely unfounded, for the time being at least. There, the main working population aged between 15 and 59 is expected to continue to grow during the next 45 years. Only after 2015 is it predicted that the number of people aged 60 and above will become larger than the number of children aged 15 and below.

Europe is another matter, however. Here the demographic bomb has already exploded, although its effects are yet to be fully appreciated. In Europe, the number of people aged 60-plus overtook the number of children in 1995. By 2050, Europe will have twice as many older people as children. Looking to the future, only the older population is predicted to increase. Across the EU, the number of workers aged between 50 and 64 will increase by 25 per cent in the next two decades, whereas the number aged between 20 and 29 will drop by 20 per cent.

It is a similar picture in many of the developing regions. In Asia, the number of people aged 60 plus will overtake the number of children by 2040, and the population aged 15 to 59 is expected to peak and then decline. It is a similar picture in Latin America. Only in Africa is the number of children expected to outnumber the ageing population for some time to come.

These demographic trends are likely to have a very profound effect on society and on work. As the size of the traditional working population declines, so more people will be expected or choose to work into their old age. Plus, many people are living longer. Some predictions suggest that, by 2074, 1.2 million Britons will reach 100, with over-80s increasing by 50 per cent in the first quarter of this century to 3.5 million.

The solution is likely to be a concerted effort to increase the childbirth rate, as well as extending the retirement age. That retirement 'round the world trip' may be further away than you thought.

103.   Is Chinese the business language of the future?

Conducting business in different languages is costly. Just ask officials at the European Union.

The EU is home to over 450 million Europeans, with a diverse ethnic and cultural background. Understandably, they speak many different languages – there are 25 member states, and 20 languages.

And, in the spirit of diversity, the EU accords equal status to its official languages, allowing each member state to address the EU in its mother tongue. Furthermore, the EU insists that countries seeking accession to the EU protect minority language rights. Good news for speakers of minority languages, such as Romany and Ruthenian, who fear for the survival of their language.

But at what cost, this protection of linguistic diversity? The EU requires the employment of over 470 translators and, in 2005, it translated 1,324,231 pages of material. The translation budget for 2006 was €800 million. In 2007, this figure is expected to rise to €830 million as Bulgaria and Romania join the EU and the organisation moves towards its target of employing 60 translators for each language. In an effort to reduce costs, only meetings of EU leaders and ministers are translated into all official languages. Lower-level meetings will be translated into a few of the major languages.

The language challenges presented by the EU are just a microcosm of those presented by globalisation. English may be the *lingua franca* of international business in 2008, but what about the billion or so Mandarin speakers in China, the world's fastest growing superpower? Or the third of a billion Spanish speakers, or 200 million or so Arabic speakers?

The obvious solution to the costs of doing business in a variety of languages across the globe is to adopt a single, universal business language. Such solutions, however, tend not to be popular.

In 1887, in an admirable attempt to reduce conflict between neighbouring communities of Poles, Russians and Germans, Ludovic Zamenhof published details of a new language using the pseudonym Doktoro Esperanto. Esperanto, as the language became known, was later described by the US government as a 'neutral interlanguage ... not identifiable with any alliance or ideology' and 'far easier to learn and use than any national language.'

Despite its obvious qualifications, Esperanto never became a universal language. Ultimately, as remains the case today, nationalism prevailed. For example, a move to have the language adopted by the League of Nations was blocked by France, who subsequently banned the language from its schools. Josef Stalin called it 'that dangerous language'. Governments across Central Europe obstructed use of the language. Esperanto speakers were persecuted in some countries, and even shot.

104.   Are you feeling guilty?

Counterfeit goods and business crime, eh? That's slightly shifty market traders offering you surprisingly cheap Rolex watches, and teenage music fans download-ing loud noisy indie music from other teenage music fans, who've ripped it into MP3 files and are now sharing it with the world via a peer-to-peer (P2P) network, right? How bad can that be?

If only it were that simple. From counterfeiting to digital piracy, the legitimate business of corporations is threatened by an ever-increasing erosion of intel-lectual property rights.

Estimates of the value of counterfeit goods vary. For a start, they are based on intelligence from goods seizures, and the quality of information varies from country to country. However, to give some idea of the scale of the problem, in 2006, according the Gieschen Consultancy, there were seizures and losses with a total value of US$1.9 billion. That is more than the GDP of 29 countries, includ-ing Belize, Sierre Leone, the Gambia, the Seychelles and St. Lucia. The seizures and losses involved 1647 global incidents of intellectual property theft, focusing exclusively on copyright and trademark infringement, in 92 countries.

Digital piracy is rife. US-based consumer research firm NPD reported that the number of US households actively downloading music from P2P sites grew from an estimated 6 million in 2004 to 14.9 million in 2006. P2P networks were responsible for five billion downloads in 2006 alone. Global music sales are down by over a quarter over the last five or so years.

Countries are not immune from bad business practice. In December 2006, at a UN anti-corruption conference in Jordan, Jordanian Prime Minister, Marouf al-Bakhit, said that global corruption had reached 'unprecedented levels', and quoted World Bank figures that put bribery at US$1 trillion (€750 million) annually.

For anyone thinking of doing business abroad, it is worth checking the global ranking of bribe payers – an index of those countries where companies are per-ceived as most likely to indulge in corrupt business practices such as bribery. The worst offenders, according to Transparency International's International *2006*

Bribe Payers Index, were India, China, and Russia. Not far off, were countries like Turkey, an EU candidate.

105.   Are you talking about the Y Generation?

Generation X refers to people born in the 1960s and 1970s; they are the demographic group that came after the baby boomers. The phrase was used by Charles Hamblett and Jane Deverson in 1964 in their novel *Generation X*, which portrayed the children who would come of age in the closing years of the 20th century. However, its usage became widespread in the late 1980s and early 1990s following Douglas Coupland's 1991 book *Generation X: tales for an accelerated culture*.

Coupland has described Generation X as a 'way of looking at the world' rather than a chronological age. Defining characteristics of Generation Xers include apathy, lack of direction and a cynical outlook on life, but also the strong desire for a settled life and a healthy respect for the benefit of a college education. Generation Xers are also referred to as the slacker generation and the MTV generation.

On the heels of Gen. X is Generation Y, also known as the Millennium Generation and Echo Boomers. Gen. Y is the US generation produced by the baby boom between a period variously described as 1979 to 1994 or 1980 to 1996, even to 2000. Generation Y is three times the size of Generation X, and close to the 72 million of the original baby boomers. Between the years 2010 and 2020, Generation Y will make up 41 per cent of the US population.

Generation Y appears to have adjusted to the new working landscape, and comes equipped with a new set of values. Two obvious examples of this shift in attitude are the increasing numbers of young people heading for careers as entrepreneurs, as well as a work-to-live mentality, rather than the live-to-work mentality common among members of Gen. X. Generation Y has little concept of, or interest in, the old 9-to-5, five days a week, full-time working patterns.

106. Do you know a good slogan when you hear one?

'Drink Coca-Cola.' With these words, Dr John Stith Pemberton launched Coca-Cola on an unsuspecting public in 1886. As slogans go, Pemberton's pithy exhortation is about as direct as it gets. Yet, 100-plus years and 60-plus slogans later, that brief instruction still rates as classic.

An effective slogan says a thousand words, or it should do in the hands of a skilled copywriter. Slogans play an essential role in marketing, and product and service awareness in particular. In his book, *Creative Advertising*, Charles Whittier describes a slogan:

'A slogan should be a statement of such merit about a product or service that it is worthy of continuous repetitive advertising; is worthwhile for the public to remember; and is phrased in such a way that the public is likely to remember it.'

Coca-Cola has extolled the virtues of a fizzy drink in more ways than would seem possible. Over the years, from the minds of various marketers and copy-writers, we have had: 'Enjoy a glass of liquid laughter'; 'Coca-Cola is the shortest distance between thirst and refreshment'; 'It's the real thing'; 'Have a Coke and a smile'; 'Always Coca-Cola'; and many more.

Politics and propaganda are also fans of the slogan. 'Labour isn't working'; 'Ask not what your country can do for you – ask what you can do for your country';

'Tough on crime, tough on the causes of crime'; 'Speak softly and carry a big stick'[1] – all examples of the political spin-masters at work.

One problem with a slogan is knowing when to change it. Quite often, the temptation is to change a slogan too soon, just as the public become familiar with it. Maxwell House coffee's slogan 'Good to the last drop' was invented in 1915 and is still used today.

One legendary story has it that, when a senior executive in Pepsi decided it was time for a new jingle, they asked the ad agency account manager how many people were working on the account. Told that it was 55 people, the executive demanded to know what they all did. One, he was told, is working on ideas for a new jingle; the other 54 are tasked with making sure the old one isn't changed.

In the Advertising Slogan Hall of Fame (www.adslogans.co.uk/hof), the following slogans were the first ten to be admitted. See how many you can connect to the company (some are obviously easier than others):

'We try harder';
'Go to work on an egg';
'Guinness is good for you';
'Don't be vague. Ask for Haig';
'Happiness is a cigar called Hamlet';
'Heineken refreshes the parts other beers cannot reach';
'Beanz Meanz Heinz';
'It is. Are you?';
'Just do it';
'Think small'.[2]

---

[1] Conservative Election slogan, 1997; JF Kennedy speech, 1961; Tony Blair as Shadow Home Secretary, 1994; Theodore Roosevelt in a letter, 1900.

[2] Avis; Egg Marketing Board; Guinness; Haig Scotch Whisky; Hamlet; Heineken; Heinz; *The Independent*; Nike; Volkswagen.

107. What is scenario planning?

Cost accounting is all very well, poring over historical cost trends in an effort to improve profitability. But, as the investment health warnings never tire of telling us, values can go down as well as up, and the future is unpredictable.

What if, though, it were possible to divine the future – or at least to imagine the possibilities? As it turns out, the future isn't that unpredictable, and is certainly not unimaginable. For some time now, many of the world's leading organisations have learned to think the unthinkable using scenario planning, a technique developed in the 1950s, which involves creating alternative stories, or scenarios, about how the future might pan out.

The concept was created at the RAND Corporation, a US-based global policy think tank, during the 1950s and 1960s. Military strategist, Herman Kahn, and social scientist, Leo Rosten, developed techniques enabling them to model possible scenarios such as a potential thermonuclear strike. The idea was that creating stories about the future would help people escape the shackles of existing mental models and contemplate 'unthinkable' futures, allowing them to plan for the unexpected. In this case, a heating up of the Cold War.

During the 1970s, a scenario-planning team was formed at Royal Dutch/Shell. The team pushed its scenario planning well beyond the usual five-year strategic-plan horizon. Shell's scenario-planning experiment was a huge success. After the Yom Kippur war, the oil embargo caught most companies by surprise. Shell, though, had considered the impact of an increase in oil price and managed to avoid the worst shocks. In 1982, Shell's scenario planners speculated that oil prices could collapse to $16 a barrel. They also foresaw the collapse of the Soviet Union, years before it happened.

While many more organisations engage in scenario planning today, it is still viewed as too sci-fi by some. Scenario planning is not a 'sit around and have a chat about the future' process, though. It has a clearly defined structure that includes important sounding activities such as: task analysis, influence analysis and consequence analysis. Structured corporate crystal-ball gazing.

108.   Why should I care about Web 2.0?

Time magazine is famous for its annual Person of the Year award. In December 2006, *Time* proclaimed that year's winner: 'It's you.' Congratulations. You now make up part of an illustrious – and not so illustrious – group of individuals that includes George W. Bush (three times winner), Bill Clinton (twice), F.D. Roosevelt, Winston Churchill, Hitler and Josef Stalin.

The reason we all got the vote in 2006 was that Web 2.0, the second coming of the internet, is driven by the millions of people across the world who log on to websites like Photobucket, Flickr, Facebook, MySpace, YouTube and LinkedIn, and fill up their pages with content. Communities of users create content, sucking in the eyeballs, they rate, police, and best of all, market the sites.

What is Web 2.0? According to Wikipedia, the user-generated online encyclopaedia, 'Web 2.0 refers to a perceived or proposed second generation of internet-based services – such as social networking sites, wikis [user-editable websites], communication tools and folksonomies [user tagging] – that emphasise online collaboration and sharing among users.'

But what relevance, if any, does Web 2.0 have for the corporate world? Doubters of Web 2.0's impact on the wider business world should note the tale of Lonelygirl15. In the summer of 2006, one of the most watched people on YouTube and MySpace was Bree, a sixteen-year-old, home-educated girl – also known as Lonelygirl15. Millions tuned in to watch video clips of the shy but precocious Bree, talking about a range of subjects that included the Tolstoy principle, turtles, Heisenberg's uncertainty principle and Purple Monkey.

As viewer numbers climbed steadily, rumours surfaced that all was not as it should be in the lonelygirl universe. The slick editing and production values, said conspiracists, hinted at something more commercial than a teenager's amateur video diary.

Sure enough, Bree was outed as the not so lonely Jessica Rose, 19, formerly of the New York Film Academy (LA branch). The filmmakers were California-based twentysomethings Miles Beckett, Mesh Flinders, and Greg Goodfried, signed with top Hollywood talent agents, Creative Artists Agency. The whole home video diary thing was a charade – albeit an extremely popular one.

The part of the lonelygirl story that demands the attention of corporate marketers is the consumer response to unfolding events. Lonelygirl15 was the all-time number one video channel on YouTube, with over 15 million cumulative page views, and with audience interaction helping to stir up attention and shape the lonelygirl story. When it comes to marketing to Generation Y –the internet generation – forget conventional, traditional media. Magazines, papers and television have their place, but the internet is where it is really at.

109.   Does something smell fishy?

You nip into the superstore after work to buy a few things for supper, and are greeted by the comforting smell of freshly baked bread. But hold on a minute: the bread was baked at the crack of dawn while you were safely tucked up in bed, so what is going on?

Of course, it is all part of an attempt to manipulate consumer behaviour. The superstores are past masters at appealing to the subconscious shopper in you. It starts with the store layout. Greeted by the cheering sight of fresh fruit and vegetables in naturally lit displays, rather than row upon row of tin cans, you have to make your way to the back of the store to get the grocery staples, like milk and bread. The hope is that you make a few impulse purchases along the way.

Smell is increasingly being used as marketing weapon by retailers too. Samsung, for example, uses a fragrance that smells like honeydew melon in some of its US electronic stores. Mobile-phone company Sony Ericsson has launched a mobile phone that smells not of nasty plastic, but of a soothing aroma, depending on which of 11 replaceable scented sheets you use. LG Electronics used a chocolate fragrance with the packaging for its LG Chocolate mobile phones. British Airways, apparently, helps to create a pleasant atmosphere in its lounges using the smell of freshly cut grass.

It's not all the sweet smell of marketing, however. Researchers found that the smell of underarm sweat encouraged men to buy magazines – or at least

Men's Health. Try not to go to the newsagents straight after the gym, or you may end up penniless.

And other research casts doubt on the advisability of superstores assaulting our 1000 olfactory genes, capable of detecting about 10,000 distinct scents, with the smell of fresh bread. A study on driving and smells in the US revealed that the smell of fast food wrappers, fresh bread or pastry can cause driver irritability, and an increased chance of involvement in road rage. Next time you see an angry shopper waving a baguette, keep your distance – it could be aroma-induced superstore rage.

110. What is the most valuable brand?

With a value of US$67,000 million, the brand heading up the 2006 Interbrand annual survey of the world's most valuable brands was Coca-Cola. In fact, the top five brands were the same as in 2005: Coca-Cola, Microsoft, IBM, General Electric and Intel.

The meteoric rise of Google continued with the search company jumping 14 places from 38 to 24. Heading in the other direction was Ford, falling eight places from 22 to 30. It's a sad story of decline for a brand that was ranked at eight in the first Interbrand most valuable brand survey in 2001. Another big faller in the 2006 survey was fashion brand Gap, down 12 from 40 to 52.

As you might imagine, measuring the value of a brand is quite a challenge, given that it is largely intangible. Interbrand uses a combination of metrics. The three core components are: financial analysis – forecasted and current revenue that can be directly attributed to a brand; role of brand analysis – how the brand influences customer demand at the point of purchase; and brand strength analysis – a benchmark of the brand's ability to secure ongoing customer demand, involving factors like brand loyalty.

The Interbrand survey is a useful guide to global business trends and rising corporate stars. Google was nowhere to be seen on the 2001 list, but has made dramatic progress since, whereas Barbie (and presumably Ken) has vanished from the list – it was 84th in 2001 – in the face of competition from the sassy Bratz dolls.

111.   Is your mission impossible?

A corporate mission statement is intended to encapsulate the essence of the organisation's purpose, its *raison d'être*. It is a rallying cry, uniting the employees in a common cause. At the same time, it acts as a message for the external world, a signal to the world, to potential consumers and other stakeholders, of what the organisation stands for. In an ideal world, it captures the spirit of, enhances, and reinforces the brand.

That's in an ideal world. In reality, it is a hard task to write a great mission statement. For many wordsmiths over the years, refining the proposition has proved a tough challenge. Take one of the earliest mission statements, that of the Ringling Brothers Circus, circa 1900:

'To be good, mankind must be happy. To wreathe the faces of humanity in smiles for a time, to loosen the chains that hold man captive to his duties and return him to them better fitted for his obligations is the mission of amusement. Amusement unfetters the mind from its environs and changes the dreary monotony of the factory's spindles to the joyous song of the meadowlark ...' etc., etc.

More modern corporations have also struggled to contain the message into a bite-size form. IBM got the word count down a bit, but still ended up on the long side:

'At IBM, we strive to lead in the invention, development and manufacture of the industry's most advanced information technologies, including computer systems, software, storage systems and microelectronics. We translate these advanced technologies into value for our customers through our professional solutions, services and consulting businesses worldwide.'

A popular option is the one-liner (note: this is not the same as an advertising slogan). This may be followed by a list of values. In the 1950s, for example, Sony wanted to 'become the company most known for changing the worldwide poor-quality image of Japanese products.' Ford Motor Company proclaimed at the beginning of the 20th century: 'Ford will democratise the automobile.' The Minnesota-based 3M, a company famous for its innovation, has a mission statement about making known unknowns: 'To solve unsolved problems innovatively.'

For the mission-statementless, personal or corporate, who lack the resources to hire a consultant to craft a mission statement, try an online mission generator instead:

www.dilbert.com/comics/dilbert/games/career/bin/ms.cgi or

www.netinsight.co.uk/portfolio/mission/missgen.asp

112. Do Skunk Works work?

As corporations grow larger, kindling the entrepreneurial fires of innovation becomes more difficult. Some companies have tried to cultivate pockets of inspiration within the organisation by allowing workers to hive off small teams and do their own thing.

So if you fancy disappearing off into the nooks and crannies of the organisation you work for, together with a few mates, hijacking a budget, and having some fun innovating for a few months or longer, here is the information you need to justify it to your bosses.

During World War II, US intelligence got news of a new development by Germany's war machine – the jet fighter. The US military, forced into playing catch-up, tasked Lockheed with developing a jet fighter for the US airforce.

Clarence L. 'Kelly' Johnson, Lockheed's leading engineer, promised to develop a prototype within 180 days; it was a very tough challenge. Johnson gathered together 23 engineers and 103 shop mechanics from various other projects, snaffled a small assembly shed in Lockheed's Burbank, California plant, and worked ten hours a day, six days a week until, after 143 days, they had built the XP-80 prototype jet.

This stand-alone project was christened Skunk Works. There are various stories of where the name came from. Johnson said that, when outsiders asked what was going on in the assembly shed, they would be told Johnson and his team were stirring up a brew – kickapoo juice. From there, it was a short leap of the imagination to Al Capp's 'Li'l Abner' comic strip, in which Hillbillies added skunks to the pot when brewing up some strong kickapoo moonshine.

Skunk Works were later popularised by management guru and bestselling author Tom Peters in *In Search of Excellence*, and the concept was adopted by companies such as IBM and Apple.

The Skunk Works concept has long since been pored over and dissected, to discover the secrets of its success. Once you have persuaded the boss to hand over the money and the location, there are a number of key factors you need to pay attention to. These include: making sure the team has the necessary power to drive the project forward; plenty of advance planning; focusing on the task in hand; and not adhering to the organisational orthodoxy.

Happy innovating.

Section 8:
Breaking free

- How do you know if your business idea is inspired or crazy?
- Have you got a handle on your promo?
- How risky is starting a business?
- What makes a good logo?
- Have you seen your boss lately?
- What is the value of values?
- What is the tipping point?
- Could you be your own boss?
- Is it too late to start a new career?
- What's in a name?
- Where do great business ideas come from?
- How much money do you need?
- What did Steve Jobs, Bill Hewlett and Walt Disney have in common?
- What is an elevator pitch?
- Feeling philanthropic?
- Why 128 questions?

113.   How do you know if your business idea is inspired or crazy?

The short answer: you don't. Not with any certainty. The most unlikely idea can turn out to be a huge success. Who, for example, would have predicted that it was possible to get rich by selling pebbles in small boxes? But that is exactly what Gary Dahl did in 1975.

Former advertising executive Dahl founded Rock Bottom Productions, and sold pebbles to the American public as pets. Pet Rocks retailed at US$3.95, and came in a brown cardboard box, in the style of a pet carrier. Also included was a training manual, dealing with issues such as how to tell if your pet rock was feeling unwell and obedience training.

Pet rocks were the height of novelty gift fashion for about six months, although, like all fads, they were soon little more than a fond memory. The pebbles were so popular that they made Dahl a millionaire.

On the other hand, a personal transportation device that is cheap to run and doesn't involve expending large amounts of pedal power, or getting knocked down by careless motorists, sounds like a reasonable idea. A brilliant idea, even. Unfortunately, as the device in question was the Sinclair C5, it turned out not to be such a successful idea after all. Launched in January 1985, the C5 was a battery-assisted tricycle, partly designed by Lotus, the sports car manufacturer, and built by Hoover, which makes washing machines, cookers and vacuum cleaners.

Had the idea been pitched on BBC's business idea show *Dragons' Den*, the Dragons might have commented on the possible dangers involved in driving a vehicle in busy traffic, with a top speed of 15 miles per hour, and a driving position a few inches off the ground. Or they might have pointed out that, with no roof, it may not have been designed with the UK's 120 or so average days of rainfall in mind. Although some weather protection, mirrors, indicators and other add-ons were available as accessories.

In the event, overheating motors, batteries that gave out more quickly in cold weather, the sheer impractical nature of the machine plus various other problems did for the C5. At its launch, the vehicle sold for £399, but soon it was being discounted to £139 or less. Either 12,000 or 17,000 C5s were produced and sold, depending on which source you read. What is not in question is the date that the Sinclair Vehicles went into receivership – 12 October 1985.

114.   Have you got a handle on your promo?

At some point or another, we have all taken part in a product promotion. Collect the tokens from the side of your breakfast cereal and get a free bendy Tyrannosaurus Rex. Buy enough petrol and get a set of glasses, which almost, but not quite, look like crystal.

The first person believed to extensively use a promotional product was George Washington. In what appears to be a votes-for-buttons campaign, commemorative buttons were given out to the public during his 1789 election. But things don't always go to plan.

Sometimes the promotion can simply be too generous. In 1992, Hoover launched a promotion to clear some old stock from its warehouses. Spend just £100 on any Hoover product, and two return flights to Europe would be yours.

What made things worse for Hoover was that it was slow to realise that it had made a gigantic miscalculation. Even as it was struggling to cope with the initial offer, it launched a second, this time to the US. Hoover was overwhelmed and, as the press began to look into the deal, it began to receive a flood of bad publicity, which in itself made the offer still more popular.

Questions were asked in Parliament and soon people began to take Hoover to court as it failed to deliver on its promises. Eventually, about 220,000 people did fly, but it ended up costing the company £48 million.

In 1996, the TV commercials for the 'Pepsi Stuff' promotion featured various items that could be obtained in exchange for Pepsi Points. Pepsi Points were obtained through purchasing Pepsi products, or, if you took time to read the fine print, could be purchased for ten cents each. At the end of one of the TV commercials, a teenager was shown arriving at school in a Harrier Jet with a line saying, 'Harrier Jet, seven million Pepsi Points.'

John Leonard of Seattle accumulated 15 actual Pepsi Points and submitted them along with a cheque for $700,008.50 to purchase the balance of Pepsi Points he needed for the Harrier Jet. The extra money was for the $10.00 shipping and handling costs as stipulated in the promotion contest rules. When Pepsi failed to deliver the jet, Mr Leonard sued, but eventually lost his court battle.

115. How risky is starting a business?

To begin with, the start-up failure statistics are not encouraging. About 15 per cent of new businesses fail within their first year, and Small Business Service figures show that 30 per cent of businesses fail after three years.

Despite all the stories about rich, famous entrepreneurs and their fast expensive luxurious lifestyles, sparking a heavy bout of entrepreneur envy, for every Richard Branson, Donald Trump or Bill Gates there are countless washed-up, failed or doggedly-determined-but-never-quite-succeeding almost business titans.

Entrepreneurs walk a thin tightrope between success and failure. Many fall, sometimes repeatedly, but get back up again before making good. Others, though, never make it back. You can have a brilliant idea, even a very successful business, but if you put one step wrong, you risk being punished with swift and very final failure.

Sir Freddie Laker is a great example of the vagaries of entrepreneurship. Laker started his own airline, Laker Airways, in 1966. Then, in 1977, he founded Laker Skytrain. It was the first cut-price transatlantic airline, and came way before budget airlines like RyanAir and EasyJet. Unfortunately, the competition wasn't so impressed with Sir Freddie's business and, after a vicious price war, Laker Airways went bust in 1982, to the tune of £270 million.

Further back in time and the sorry tale of engineer Stuart Cramer is another lesson to would-be entrepreneurs. Willis Haviland Carrier is the man credited with bringing climate control to the fingertips of millions of sweltering Americans.

Carrier perfected air-conditioning, filed patents, and rolled out air-conditioning across the US through his company, the Carrier Engineering Corporation.

But Carrier didn't invent the term. That honour goes to Stuart Cramer of Charlotte, North Carolina. Educated at the United States Naval Academy and the Columbia University School of Mines, Cramer trained as an engineer, and built up substantial holdings in the textile industry of the southern states in the early 1900s. He designed a device to moisten the air in his textile factories, and filed a patent for 'The Cramer System of Air Conditioning.' At a convention of cotton manufacturers in 1906, he said, 'I have used the term "air conditioning" to include humidifying and air cleaning and heating and ventilation.'

Cramer's problem was lack of vision. Great entrepreneurs think big; the Parks-Cramer Company, however, thought cotton industry, rather than America. Carrier's more expansive plans for air conditioning mean that his name and not Cramer's lives on in the list of great 20th century entrepreneurs.

But, if things look bleak in the early days, don't despair. It is possible to snatch victory from the jaws of defeat. In 1977, Full Compass Systems Ltd., a Middleton, Wisconsin dealer of audio, video and lighting equipment, opened for business. In its first year, it was burgled twice, had its insurance cancelled and got to the point where the owners couldn't afford the rent.

In a last-ditch attempt to save the business, owners Jonathan and Susan Lipp asked their teenage sons for help. The boys pooled their *bar mitzvah* money and invested $500 each in the company. By 1999, the company had grown to 150 employees and posted annual revenue of $45 million.

116. What makes a good logo?

A red circle with a broad blue band going through it: it's a simple logo that has come to be synonymous with London. The London Underground logo, or roundel, as it is properly called, was re-designed by Edward Johnston in 1918, when he replaced the original solid red circle with a red hoop. It's simple, effective and has stood the test of time.

Logos are another way of generating goodwill among customers when building a brand. They help a business stand out from the crowd. They can sometimes become so recognisable that they embody the values that a business subscribes to. What's more, they needn't cost a fortune. In 1971, Caroline Davidson created the Nike swoosh, for which she received $35. Of course, you might choose to pay more than £400,000 for your logo as the organising committee for the London 2012 Olympics did.

A successful logo has a number of elements.

- *Professionalism*. The logo needs to embody the professional nature of the enterprise. Humorous logos may make potential customers smile, but do they suggest quality and professionalism?
- *Colour*. A study conducted by the University of Chicago in 1907 concluded that the easiest colour to spot was yellow, and it was this fact that encouraged John Hertz, the founder of the Yellow Cab Company, to paint all his cabs yellow. It also suggests why 75 per cent of the pencils sold in America are painted yellow. And why bananas are so popular. To help keep your costs down, it is generally better to have no more than two colours in a logo. A logo can still make a big impact without the expense of full-colour printing on all the

materials – for example, the yellow 'M' on the red background that constitutes the McDonalds mark.

- *Reproduction*. A logo needs to appear on a variety of different media and in a host of different sizes. Does it look equally good on letterheaded paper as it on a billboard poster or TV? The colour should look the same wherever the logo appears. With a designer-produced logo, always ask for the Pantone reference for any colours, to reduce the chances of discrepancies.

Devising a logo that achieves all of the things mentioned here can take some time. It is worth carrying a notebook for those moments when inspiration strikes, possibly when stuck on a platform somewhere deep in the belly of the London Underground.

117.   Have you seen your boss lately?

The chances are that your manager has read about MBWA – management by walking about (or wandering about) – probably in a 'how to manage' book.

MBWA is a way for managers to keep in touch with what is going on at different levels of the organisation. By visiting the shop floor or offices where the general staff work, and talking to employees, managers can cut through organisational hierarchies. In other words, they can see how messy your desk is, and catch you surfing the internet when you should be writing that report.

The next time your boss startles you by sidling up unannounced when you are halfway through a cream cake and making company small talk, blame Walter Packard. During the 1970s, management hierarchies were far more rigid than they are today. The management and the workforce had little to do with each other. Managers had their own dining room, car park, even lift. If they were lucky, they might not bump into an employee for days, if not weeks.

At Hewlett-Packard, though, Packard liked to wander around the workforce and find out what was happening. It motivated the workforce – Packard was actually interested enough in them to talk to them and get their opinions. Packard's approach was picked up and popularised in the bestselling management book *In Search Of Excellence* in 1985.

Packard was not the first CEO to venture out in this way, though. In the 1930s, Konosuke Matsushita, CEO and founder of Matsushita Corporation (Panasonic is one of its brands) was also a great believer in walking the floor – and not only of his factories. Matsushita would also do the rounds of department stores, visiting each electric appliance department, with one of his managers trailing behind handing out business cards.

Airline owners Richard Branson and Stelios Haji-Ioannou take the concept one step further by practicing managing by flying about. They are both frequent passengers on their own airlines and will regularly canvass the opinions of both staff and passengers.

118.   What is the value of values?

When Jack Welch was CEO at General Electric, he carried a laminated card in his pocket. On the card were written GE's corporate values. For the employees, failure to live those values was grounds for dismissal. At one meeting Welch surprised his audience saying: 'Look around you: there are five fewer officers here than there were last year. One was fired for the numbers, four were fired for values.'

At GE, Welch explicitly linked the performance of its managers to the company's values. Some 5000 GE employees took part in the debate about the company's values over a three-year period. In 1989, an early draft of the values statement urged staff to embrace the GE values. Those who did not, Welch suggested, might fare better elsewhere. 'Individuals whose values do not coincide with these expressed preferences will more likely flourish better outside the General Electric Company,' the statement read. It became known as the 'flourish off' statement, and caused such an outcry that it was dropped from the final values statement.

Why bother with corporate values? Because, with less management to tell them what to do, employees are encouraged to take decisions themselves. The challenge for the company is to ensure that decisions taken by its staff reflect the company's strategy. One way they can do this is by providing staff with a corporate version of the moral compass to guide employees in their decision-making. Hence the values.

Many companies set down their values in writing. David Packard and Bill Hewlett took the trouble to enshrine the corporate culture of Hewlett-Packard – respect for others, community, hard work – in The HP Way, written in 1957. Pharmaceutical giant Johnson & Johnson has its *Credo*, penned by founder General Robert Wood Johnson in 1943.

And values aren't some meaningless exercise – or at least they shouldn't be – as research shows that values have real value in terms of corporate performance. A four-year study by Professor John Kotter, of Harvard Business School, and colleague John Heskett, of between nine and ten firms in each of 20 industries, found that firms with a strong culture, based on a foundation of shared values, outperformed the other firms in the study by a huge margin.

The companies with values saw their revenues grow over four times more quickly; the rate of job creation was seven times higher; the stock price grew twelve times faster; and profit performance was 750 per cent higher.

119.   What is the tipping point?

What if you could take an idea about a product or service and, with the help of just a few people, see it spread throughout the world? No need for huge advertising budgets, TV ads, or big marketing departments.

It may sound too good to be true but, according to the ideas in Malcolm Gladwell's influential book *The Tipping Point*, it is possible. Gladwell is a staff wruter with *The New Yorker*. In *The Tipping Point*, Gladwell observes how fashions take hold, noting that 'ideas and products and messages and behaviours spread just like viruses do.'

A few people act as carriers, spreading the cultural infection; the idea takes hold, spreads more rapidly, and, at a tipping point, reaches critical mass. The spread of information in this way is examined in Seth Godin's book *Unleashing the Idea Virus*.

The concept of the tipping point would be less significant were it not for advances in communications technology, which allow information to be rapidly propagated across the globe. This promulgation of ideas creates some significant problems for organisations and individuals, in particular managing the risks related to so called 'infodemics' – information epidemics.

As recent pandemic scares demonstrate, advances in ICT technology can lead to global Chinese whispers as rumours reverberate around the world at high speed.

With the SARS epidemic weighing on the world, David Rothkopf, a visiting scholar at the Carnegie Endowment for International Peace, wrote an article in the *Washington Post* in 2003, in which he described the phenomenon of the 'infodemic': 'a few facts, mixed with fear, speculation and rumour, amplified and relayed swiftly worldwide by modern information technologies.' Information outbreaks are, he noted, complex creatures driven by a range of factors, an intermingling of mainstream and specialist media.

If the situation was challenging in 2003, it is all the more pressing today. Messages via blogs, podcasts, broadsheets, TV stations, radio stations, email, fax, texting and mobile phones, in a multitude of languages, coalesce to create a miasma of fact and speculation that can cost corporations millions of dollars, and individuals their careers and reputations. All companies, and individuals (try Googling your name: you may be surprised at what you discover) should monitor the official and unofficial media, and see how information is being interpreted. If you don't control the message, someone else will.

120. Could you be your own boss?

Not everyone is cut out to be Bill Gates or Richard Branson. Many more people are turning to entrepreneurship as a way out of the wage slavedom of conventional corporate life. But it takes a certain set of qualities to be a successful entrepreneur.

Core business skills are a must. Sure, a few get by on a wing and a prayer. But most successful entrepreneurs have a fairly good grasp of the business basics: operations, marketing, finance, strategy and IT. What they don't know, they find out, in what is usually a very steep learning curve – more a learning cliff, really.

If the founder doesn't know something, they team up with someone who does. That's why many successful businesses are the product of two minds rather than one, whether it is Bill Gates and Paul Allen, Steve Wozniak and Steve Jobs, or Dave Packard and Bill Hewlett.

Why do you need to know the business stuff? Because, at the start, and sometimes all the way through, it is hands on for the business founder(s). Then, when it ceases to be quite as hands on, you need to be sure other people are not taking you for an expensive ride.

As well as business skills and knowledge, an entrepreneur also needs other attributes, including: excellent communication skills, adaptability, negotiation skills, the ability to work in a team and to motivate others and networking skills.

Perhaps two of the most important, and linked, attributes, however, are persistence and unbridled optimism. Most successful entrepreneurs encounter failure and disappointment on the road to success, but they shrug it off and carry on, certain in the knowledge that they will eventually succeed.

James Dyson, for example, was nearly bankrupted as he was forced to pay substantial fees to renew his patents each year, even before his revolutionary Dual Cyclone vacuum cleaner came to market. During the development years, he risked everything and, fortunately for him, the risk paid off.

121.   Is it too late to start a new career?

With the right mindset, it is rarely too late to start a new career. In fact, many career changers have had spectacular success with second or even third careers – far more so than on the path they originally began with.

Ray Kroc was a late starter. After a lengthy and unremarkable career as a milk-shake mixer salesman, Kroc was looking forward to a comfortable retirement, when he walked into a small hamburger restaurant in San Bernardino, California in 1954.

The restaurant was owned and run by the McDonald brothers, and Kroc was impressed by what he saw. He cut himself a deal with the brothers, bought into the business, drew up a set of rules governing the operation of new McDonald's restaurants, and set about creating a franchise network.

By 1963, Kroc had bought the brothers out for $2.1 million, the company had notched up one billion burgers, and restaurant number 500 was open for business. The company went public in 1965, and Kroc's $2.1 million investment soon became a $500 million fortune. Kroc splashed out on a few treats, including the San Diego Padres baseball club.

Another successful career changer took a more meandering route to business success. One of the greatest advertising executives of all time, David Ogilvy, headed for Paris after Oxford University. In the city of lights, he worked in the kitchens of the Hotel Majestic, before returning to England to work as an Aga cooker salesman. This was followed by a job in the US as a pollster for Dr George Gallup, and then a spell as a tobacco farmer with the Amish community in Lancaster County, Pennsylvania. Not the most conventional of CVs. Finally, in 1948, Ogilvy settled down to a career in advertising, founding Ogilvy & Mather. He retired in 1975, having created a business with annual billings of $800 million, and won numerous awards for his innovative advertising.

And just in case you think retirement means the end of a great business career, think again. Theodore Vail spent his life creating the American Telephone & Telegraph Company, before retiring to his 200-acre farm in Vermont. The 200 acres soon became 6000 acres, as Vail focused his energies on his new pastime.

But in 1907, the economy took a turn for the worse. Banks withdrew credit, capital dried up and stocks plummeted. Amid the economic turmoil, dark clouds gathered over the AT&T Company. Caps in hand, the directors of AT&T paid a visit to Vail's ranch in Vermont and pleaded with him to help save the company. How could he refuse?

Vail raised $21 million of new capital, followed by a quarter of a billion over the next six years. He managed the company through the financial crisis of October–November 1907, and AT&T emerged as the dominant force in telephony.

122.   What's in a name?

If being creative isn't your thing, but you are starting up a business, coming up with a new name may be an issue. Don't worry: help is at hand.

For a start, there are websites that will create business names at random. With just a couple of clicks, you can be the CEO of Zit Zit Ltd, Corategrated Capital or Xilicron. Or perhaps not.

Don't take a chance with your business name. It's important. It could set you on a journey towards greatness, or be such a burden it never allows you to get off the ground. In time, you want it to become synonymous with the product or service you are offering.

So what are the key things to consider when choosing a name? The first decision to make is whether to have a name that tells people what line of business you are in (just as once our surnames did: Smith, Cooper, Farmer, etc.) or whether to have an abstract name, to build the brand without any preconceptions.

If you choose the descriptive route, make sure that the name is appropriate. The Delicious Biscuit Company: good for selling biscuits but misleading if you are a secondhand car dealer. An abstract name has the benefit of allowing a product to stand out in a crowded market place. Häagen-Dazs is an abstract name, designed to look and sound European in a crowded American ice-cream industry. The original labels used to have an outline of Denmark, to reinforce the imaginary Scandinavian connection.

Research suggests that the letter 'k' is an advantage – Nike, Coke, etc. These names also have the benefit of being short and active-sounding, which is good for several reasons. A shorter name is more likely to be remembered. Plus it will have a better chance of becoming a verb.

Test names out on friends, family and potential customers. Do this over the phone as well as face to face. If the name can't be heard clearly over the phone, then it may well be an indication that it is not the right name for you.

Check to see if the name is available and can be trademarked. Also check to see if there is a suitable internet domain name available, and if it reads well once it is in the browser bar. There have been some spectacular oversights when it has come down to web site addresses. For example, the Experts Exchange, an information technology website, initially had its web address as www.expertsexchange.com. After some consideration, it added a hyphen in the appropriate place.

Of course you can always choose to name the business after yourself. Take the German shoemaker Adolf Dassler, who abbreviated his name and created Adidas. His brother, on the other hand, after a disagreement, set up his own sports shoe business and called it Puma.

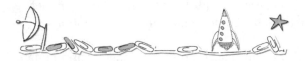

123.   Where do great business ideas come from?

Perhaps one of the most famous moments in the history of innovation happened in a bath in ancient Greece. For those who aren't already familiar with the story, the inventor and mathematician Archimedes was bathing when he had a moment of insight in which he glimpsed the truth behind the principle of floating bodies. So excited was he by this flash of genius that he ran naked into the streets of Syracuse shouting 'Eureka' (I have found it).

The Eureka moment is highly prized in the modern business world. Indeed, as many articles and books will tell you, innovation is a key factor in the competitiveness of organisations. 'Innovate or die' is the oft-quoted phrase. The corporate services sector is full of companies that teach creativeness, how to think creatively, how to be creative and how to capture creativity.

Organisations install creative rooms, comfy sofas and copious amounts of brain food in the form of chocolate and other confectionary. IDEO is an internationally successful design firm that relies on creativity to survive. The design agency nurtures a creative culture through encouraging employees to embrace chaos and challenge the orthodoxy; it facilitates the innovation process by providing prototyping material and tools to allow people to play with ideas in a physical way.

Despite all the theories about brainstorming, lateral thinking and mind maps, and other tools and techniques, the best business ideas are often the product of serendipity, happenstance and hard work.

In 1979, a Hewlett-Packard engineer found that heating ink in a certain way caused it to splatter. This discovery laid the foundations for the thermal ink-jet printer business. Willis Haviland Carrier was standing on a damp platform at Pittsburgh railway station when he was enveloped by fog. In that moment, he realised that the paradoxical solution to the problem of how to control humidity in a room lay in creating an artificial fog, in which the occupier could determine the amount of air saturation.

When a researcher created a weak adhesive at conglomerate 3M, it wasn't clear what, if any, commercial use the new invention might have. Art Fry, a chemical engineer who worked at the company, but sang in a choir in his spare time, was looking for a way to mark pages in his hymnal – paper bookmarks just fell out. So he used the weak adhesive to temporarily attach a bookmark to different pages. Then he used it to stick paper on a report when he was marking it.

The public was slow to catch on, as no one knew what to use them for. Once company representatives explained, however, there was no stopping the success of the small sticky pieces of paper.

Then again, when it comes to brilliant business ideas, it may just help to be a little bit mad. Jacob Schick, the US-born inventor of the electric razor, is said to have believed that, by shaving correctly every day, a man could live to 120. Schick died in 1937, aged 59.

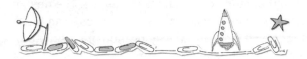

124. How much money do you need?

Legally forming a limited company in the UK will cost you somewhere between £50 and £150. That won't get you very far with your business, though. Trading requires money: to buy goods or raw materials, tools, office equipment, marketing and maybe even pay some wages.

Some of the most successful businesses, however, have been started with very little money. Walt Disney started business with $500 borrowed from his uncle, $200 from his brother Roy and $2500 from his parents, who mortgaged their house to raise the money.

Hewlett-Packard was founded in 1939 with just $538 of capital. In the spring of 1923, Raymond Rubicam founded ad agency Young & Rubicam, starting with just $5000 and one client, Quick Tipper, a company that sold a tool for capping shoelaces.

Herb Kelleher drew up a business plan for Southwest Airlines on the back of a paper napkin. Kelleher put in $10,000 and the company was incorporated in March 1967. Frank Woolworth opened his first store in Utica, NY. 'The Great Five Cent Store' opened for business on a Saturday evening in February 1879 with $321 worth of five-cent goods. The first Woolworth sale was a fire shovel.

Phil Knight teamed up with track coach Bill Bowerman and founded Blue Ribbons Sports in 1964. Knight and Bowerman invested $500 each in the new company. The brand was renamed Nike in 1971. In 1886, William Crapo Durant borrowed $1500 from the bank to found the Flint Road Cart Company. Durant went on to own Buick, Chevrolet and General Motors. More recently, in 1984,

Michael Dell started the Dell Computer Corporation with just $1000 in capital. Karan Bilimoria began Cobra Beer with £20,000 worth of student debt.

At the other end of the scale, the father of the venture capital industry, Arthur Rock, raised $5.5 million of private funding on the strength of a business plan written on one and a half pages, to start a microprocessor producer – Intel.

In other words, great businesses are down to a lot more than money.

125. What do Steve Jobs, Bill Hewlett and Walt Disney have in common?

The answer is of course – a garage. Not just any garage, but a cradle of creativity, a hothouse of invention – in each case the seat of a billion-dollar business. For most of us, 'garage' is a word that brings to mind oily rags, mechanics and improbable bills for car repairs. But, for entrepreneurs, 'garage' is full of romantic notions of business success and failure, of brainstorming and creative genius.

With brother Roy, Walt Disney launched Disney Brothers Studio from his uncle's garage in North Hollywood, although he moved out into the back of a Hollywood real estate office after he sold his first animated featurette. The garage, a modest timber affair, survives: it won reprieve from demolition in 1984 and now resides at the Stanley Ranch Museum.

When Dave Packard met Bill Hewlett at Stanford University in the 1930s, Palo Alto was best known for its prunes. Not for long, though. In 1939, the two set up business – in a garage. The idea was that Packard would be a kind of rent-an-inventor. But, before long, the garage spirit of invention took over and the two began to develop a raft of crazy gadgets, including an electric shock machine to help people lose weight and an optical device to trigger automatic urinal flushing. A device for sound engineers actually made money, giving a profit of $1539 by the end of the first year. The pair moved out of the garage in 1940.

A few years later, in the 1970s, the personal computing revolution was being fashioned in a garage. Steve Jobs and Steve Wozniak designed the Apple I computer in Jobs' bedroom and constructed the prototype in his garage.

One person you might have expected to start his business in a garage was Henry Ford. The only problem was, the garage hadn't been invented. When the car became popular in the 1920s, the cars ended up in the carriage house, with the horse and buggy. Next came rented spaces in large public and private garages. Finally, with too many cars to garage, the modern concept of the garage by the house was developed.

As for Ford, he built his prototype for the Ford motor car, the Quadricycle, in his coal shed. The only problem was, he forgot about the part where you have to get the vehicle out, and had to partly dismantle the shed in order to test drive his new invention.

126. What is an elevator pitch?

In the 1980s, high concept was all the rage in Hollywood. The idea was that you could boil down the essence of a movie to a few pithy sentences. So, if scriptwriters were lucky enough to stand next to Steven Spielberg in an elevator, they could pitch a film concept to the Hollywood big-hitter before he reached his floor. One of the best ways to convey an idea in such a short space of time was by reference to existing movies, so *Alien* became *'Jaws* on a spaceship' and *Speed* was *'Die Hard* on a bus.'

Then, when the dot com boom got underway in the late 1990s, the guys – as they invariably were – who handed out the millions to get an idea off a sheet of paper and onto the internet were so time-pressed, entrepreneurs refined the elevator pitch for a new market. Now, instead of scriptwriters pitching at movie moguls, geeky would-be dot com millionaires were accosting venture capitalists from Sand Hill Road, the legendary home of VCs in Silicon Valley. Dot com networking organisations, like First Tuesday, sprang up around the world, holding regular pitch-fests.

The dot com bubble burst, sure enough, and high-concept is out of fashion in Hollywood, for the moment at least, but the elevator pitch lives on. It's standard fare for business school MBA students and participants on entrepreneurship programmes. In a literal interpretation of the elevator pitch, one management professor, at the International University of Monaco, even gets his students to refine their presentation delivery going up and down in a real lift. First floor – VC funding.

127.   Feeling philanthropic?

So what do you do when you have made all your money, whether it is on the money markets, starting up a tech company, or making some shrewd investments? In many cases the answer is, give it away, or much of it at least.

The wealthiest people on the planet are, unsurprisingly, the largest benefactors. Bill Gates, one of the world's richest men, created the $30 billion Bill &

Melinda Gates Foundation, to which he is now devoting the majority of his time. Warren Buffett, another of the planet's richest, has also taken the decision to give away 85 per cent of his Berkshire Hathaway stock over the next few years. The majority of it will go to the Bill & Melinda Gates Foundation, from where it will be distributed.

Philanthropy is nothing new. Some of history's greatest businessmen have created long-lasting foundations. Andrew Carnegie is remembered as much for his philanthropy as his steel empire. Guided by his ethical beliefs, Carnegie had already given away $350 million of his fortune before he died in 1919. His trust fund, set up 'for the improvement of mankind,' has helped to build 3000 public libraries, the Carnegie Institute of Pittsburgh, the Carnegie Institute of Technology and the Carnegie Institution of Washington.

George Eastman, founder of Eastman Kodak, started his philanthropy at home, with his own employees. In 1899, he distributed a substantial sum from his own pocket to his workforce. Then, in 1919, he handed a third of his company holdings – worth some $10 million – to his employees. At the same time, he provided the workers with retirement annuities, life insurance and disability benefits.

To the Massachusetts Institute of Technology (MIT), Eastman donated $20 million under the name of 'Mr Smith'. For years afterwards, there was intense speculation over the identity of the mysterious Mr Smith. Eastman even joined in a toast to Mr Smith at an annual MIT alumni dinner.

Some modern business titans have adopted a new approach to philanthropy. Pierre Omidyar, founder of eBay, embarked on a drive to rid himself of 99 per cent of his fortune during his lifetime, through what has been called venture philanthropy. The idea is to seed-fund causes that present a solid business plan and meet key criteria, on points such as earnings streams.

True philanthropy costs money, and your children – if you have any – might not be that impressed. However, the act of giving may well increase your overall happiness, as well as doing a lot of good. There is also the added bonus of be-ing remembered long after your demise. Not that many people will be familiar with the Yukon Gold Company, but millions know the name of the Solomon R. Guggenheim Art Museum in New York.

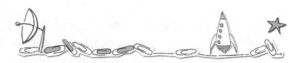

128. Why 128 questions?

No particular reason. We chose 128 questions at random, although scien-tists will tell you that random often isn't that random. And, as we didn't use a random number generator, it probably wasn't that random. (We tried that but it came up with 580.)

The truth is, we chose 127 questions, which we proceeded to answer, until, at the very end of the project, we noticed the word 'other' in the subtitle.

Some nations take more care with their choice of numbers, however. In China, certain numbers are auspicious, while others are unlucky. The number 9 means everlasting, and the pronunciation of 6 is like the word for slippery, meaning that the course of events will run smoothly.

The number most favoured by the Chinese is 8, which means prosper. So the Beijing Olympics starts at 8.00 am on the 8/8/08, and many Chinese busi-nesses have 8 in their name or multiples of 8 in their phone number. Sichuan Airlines bought the mobile number 8888 8888 for £270,000.

Unlucky numbers, according to the Chinese are 1, 4, 7 and 14.

Elsewhere in the world, however, different numbers are considered propitious and the number 7 is widely considered lucky. In casinos, 777 won the jackpot on the traditional one-armed bandit slot machines. Interestingly, in the UK lottery as of June 2007, ball number 7 was the luckiest lottery ball over the lottery's lifetime. The US and UK wedding industries had a bonanza on 7/7/07.

Unfortunately, 77 questions was not quite enough, and 777? Out of the question. While we were writing the book, we did come across some other numbers though, that just didn't seem to fit anywhere else:

- *60.7* the average retirement age in Finland
- *36,000* the distance in kilometres above the earth at which a geostationary satellite travels
- *400* the number of ounces in a standard gold bar held at Fort Knox
- *131* the number of stairways in the Pentagon
- *2618* the number of toilets at Wembley Stadium
- *7* the number of sides on a fifty pence piece
- *275* the number of stations on the London Underground
- *8* the average number of inches that Concorde would stretch as it flew across the Atlantic
- *90 million* the number of jars of Skippy peanut butter sold each year
- *1775* the number of years it would take to count all of Bill Gates money at a rate of $1 per second

Index

active listening 70–1
The Art of War 84–5
assaults, workplace 128–9
assertiveness 64–5

bank loans 114–16
best jobs in the world 2–4
billionaires 107–8
BlackBerry 26–8
  see also infomania
blogging 49–50
body language 12–13, 50–1
brainstorming 37–8
brand value 171–2
branding 157–8
bribery 163–4
budgets 148–50
bullying 63–4
burnout 142–3
business books 92–3
business cards 5–6
business expenses 111–12
business ideas 178–80, 194–5
  see also brainstorming; innovations
business names 192–4
business start-ups 182–3, 196–7
  see also innovations

careers, starting new 191–2

cars 80–2
charitable donations 56–7
compensation *see* pay
competitiveness 158–9
construction industry budgets 148–50
control 66–7
coolhunters 153–4
corporate culture 186–8
corporate perks 102–4
corporate values 186–8
  see also mission statements
corruption 163–4
counterfeiting 162–3
CrackBerry 26–8
  see also infomania
cubicles 47–9
culture, corporate 186–8
customer service 33–4
CVs 6–8
cycling 130–1

dangerous jobs 15–16
'dead wood' colleagues 73–4
delegation 66–7
demographic time bomb 159–61
desk control viii
direct marketing 146–8

elevator pitches 198–9

email bankruptcy 34–6, 140–1
emotional intelligence 68–9
employee engagement 17–19
employee innovation 131–2, 173–5
employee surveillance 59
entrepreneurship 182–3, 189–90,
        191–2
    see also innovations
expenses 111–12

family businesses 110–11
fear of work 23–4
filing systems viii
fired, being 43–4, 49–50, 54–6
first impressions 12–13
foods 40–1
football management 61–2
friends, team 61–3
fun 75–6

games 134
garages 197–8
Generations X and Y 164–5
glass ceiling 90–2
goals 46–7
golf 83–4
goodbye 43–4, 49–50, 54–6, 96–7

hacking 118–19
happiness
    money 135–6, 200–1
    work-life balance 141–2
'hara hachi bu' 41
Holocaust project ix
Hoover Dam 150
hours worked 139–40
humour 75–6

ideas, business 178–80, 194–5

    see also brainstorming; innovations
impressions, first 12–13
inbox anxiety 34–6
incompetence 76
infodemics 188–9
infomania 26–8, 34–6, 140–1
information overload 140–1
innovations
    see also brainstorming; business
            ideas
    encouraging employee 131–2, 173–5
    harmful 132–3
internet 168–70
interpersonal skills 85–6
interviews 9–10, 13–14, 16–17
inventions, harmful 132–3
investments 112–14, 116–17

jargon 155–6
job enjoyment 36–7
job market 10–12
junk mail 146–8

karoshi 142–3

languages issues 161–2
lateness excuses 136–8
laughing 75–6
leader or manager? 87–8
leadership
    customer service 33–4
    icons 150–1
    team 71–3
    theories 97–8
leaving employment 43–4, 49–50, 54–6,
        96–7
listening, active 70–1
litigation 119–20
loans 114–16

logos 184–5
lunch boxes 40–1

management by wandering about (MBWA)
     185–6
management speak 155–6
manager or leader? 87–8
manhole covers 13–14
Mayo Clinic 65
MBAs 89–90
MBWA (management by wandering about)
     185–6
meishi 6
mentors 21–2
mission statements 172–3
     see also corporate values
misunderstandings 70–1
money
     see also pay; philanthropy
     business start-ups 196–7
     happiness 135–6, 200–1
     product values 31–2
music 151–3

names, business 192–4
negotiating 31–2, 50–1
networking 20–1, 74–5, 86
niceness 85–6
numbers 201–2

'old school tie' 8–9
outsourcing 94–5

paperclips viii–ix
paperless office 154–5
Parkinson's Laws 75
pay 10–12, 106–7, 121
     see also money
perks 102–4

personal calls 29–30
personal relationships 57–8, 77–8
Peter Principle 76
philanthropy 199–201
phishing 104–5
phobias 23–4
photocopying 28–9
piracy 163
planning, scenario 167–8
power napping 67–8
PR 39–40
predictions 47–9
presentations 30–1
     see also speeches
product values 31–2
productivity 42–3
promotion, job 76, 88–9
promotions, product 180–1
publicity 39–40, 188–9

relationships, building *see* networking
relationships, personal 57–8, 77–8
role models 93–4

salaries *see* pay
scenario planning 167–8
sickies 126–7
'six degrees of separation' 57–8
Skunk Works 173–5
sleep 127–8
sleeping on the job 67–8
slogans 165–7
small world phenomenon 57–8
smell 170–1
smishing 105
South Sea bubble 116–17
speculating 116–17
speeches 30–1, 44–5
sponsoring 56–7

start-ups, business 182–3, 196–7
    see also innovations
staying power 19–20
Sun-Tzu, *The Art of War* 84–5
surveillance 59

targets 46–7
taxes 108–9
team 'dead wood' colleagues 73–4
team friendliness 61–3
team leadership 71–3
time management ix, 42–3
tipping points 188–9
trends, detecting 153–4

values
    see also mission statements
    brand 171–2

corporate 186–8
product 31–2
Vice Presidents 99–100
violence, workplace 128–9

wages *see* pay
Wall Street Crash 112–13
war, *The Art of War* 84–5
wasting company time 29–30
water cooler moments 60–1
Web 2.0 168–70
women board members 90–2
work-life balance 88–9, 139–40, 141–2
working hours 139–40
worst job in the world 124–5
worth
    finding your 10–12
    product values 31–2